PRAISE for Janet B. Mil~

The Winners' Comp

The scene Janet Milstein chose for me   ~nd was the
best I had ever seen. The scene was te~...~c, like all of Janet's
scenes. I loved performing my scene!

—SHAWN JOHNSON

I performed my scene many times, and it helped me take home
a trophy for third place! My scene also caused a lot of public-
ity for me, and I got a lot of callbacks.

—BIANCA REYES

I have read a lot of Janet Milstein's material. Her writing is real,
with real situations, not fake or phony. Her books are awesome,
and you are sure to find pieces that suit you. Students who performed her material at competitions in New York and Los An-
geles have won many awards.

—EMILY DEAK

If you were to look up the word *great* in a thesaurus, all those
words listed would describe Janet Milstein. She has been a big
factor in all of my success. She is very dedicated and passion-
ate about all of her students. Janet Milstein is the Yoda of acting coaches.

—ARRAON "SKIPPA" HIXSON

This is THE book for young actors. There is a scene for every
type of personality. Not only will the pieces stretch the actor,
but they definitely have the audience laughing. Good stuff here!

—ELLEN CRABILL, CHILDREN'S DRAMA TEACHER

I own an acting school in Atlanta and we have been using Janet's books for all of our students. If you want the best books, Janet Milstein has them all. After several years of trying to find books, I came across hers, and I have to tell you, she knows what she is doing. There aren't many books for children that are as exceptional as these.

—MILES STEPHENSON

I won first place for my piece from your book in my division. I won Top Ten in Actor of the Year. I also got seven callbacks for acting. I wanted to let you know how much I appreciated the help that you gave me in your weekend workshop. I believe that without you I would not have won nor been as confident as I was. Thank you so much for everything you've done to help me.

—TYLER HILL

Winners' Competition Series, Volume 4

~ ~ ~

Award-winning 90-Second Comic Scenes Ages 13 to 18

A Smith and Kraus Book
Published by Smith and Kraus, Inc.
177 Lyme Road, Hanover, NH 03755
www.smithandkraus.com

First Edition: June 2010
Manufactured in the United States of America
10 9 8 7 6 5 4 3 2 1

Book production by Freedom Hill Design and
Pendragon Productions
Text design by Kate Mueller
Cover design by Alex Karan, www.alexkarancreative.com
Cover photo by Alex Karan, featuring Elizabeth Cheney and Stevie Collier

ISBN-13: 978-1-57525-615-3 / 1-57525-615-0
Library of Congress Control Number: 2010928675

WINNERS' COMPETITION SERIES, VOLUME 4

Award-winning 90-Second Comic Scenes Ages 13 to 18

~ ~ ~

Edited by

JANET B. MILSTEIN

YOUNG ACTORS SERIES

A Smith and Kraus Book

CONTENTS

SCENES FOR TWO MALES

SCENES FOR ONE MALE AND ONE FEMALE

ACKNOWLEDGMENTS

This book has been the never-ending project, and I am so thankful that everyone involved has such vast reserves of patience. Short and funny has never been so long and hard! I especially commend my best friend and cowriter Barbara Lhota and my nutty—and insisting she be called beleaguered—assistant Diana Xin for putting up with my meticulousness. At least Diana got lollipops. (Don't tell Barb.) I would also like to thank the following people for their support, hard work, assistance, and belief in me:

Eric Kraus
Marisa Smith
Diana Xin
Alex Karan
Julia Gignoux
Barbara Lhota
Lindsay Price
Kate Mueller
Margaret Milstein
Natalie "Novy" Milstein
Karen "Kovy" Milstein
Amethyst Milstein
Donald Milstein
John "Tom" Miller
Karen Milstein

Joshua Milstein
Kathyrn Milstein
Melissa Milstein
Freda Milstein
Soledad Milstein
Elizabeth Cheney
Ann Cheney
Cindy Cheney
Carol Garner
Stevie Collier
Heidi Collier
Ellen Crabill
Erin Mary
Jane Hoffman
Cody

Introduction

As an acting teacher working regularly with young actors, I often have difficulty finding scenes for my students that meet my needs. To begin with, I need scenes where both characters are from the same age group. Because my students are young and class time is limited, I need scenes that are easy to memorize and work in detail within class hours. In addition, I want scenes that have a clear beginning, middle, and end, with equal opportunity for both students to shine. However, most well-plotted scenes tend to run long. What I really need are short scenes with high stakes and well-developed characters. These scenes provide the best opportunities for my students to explore concepts such as "the moment before," goals or objectives, obstacles, actions, relationship, and expectations. But when I searched for these scenes, I usually came up empty-handed and so resorted to using the same old scenes or writing my own.

This dilemma was not only happening in my beginning scene study classes, but in my on-camera classes as well. When teaching on-camera classes, especially in comedy, I need sitcom-style scenes for practice and cold reading. Scenes for television, unlike theater, are very short. Sitcom dialogue is punchy, contemporary, and clipped. The language is modern, and the pace is brisk. On camera, it is also essential to learn about hitting marks, cheating out, and spatial relations. Therefore, the shorter the scenes, the more time to practice these on-camera skills. I did not want to use scenes from actual sitcoms; I wanted the actors to approach the material without preconceived notions of how the scenes should be played.

I then tried searching through available sources of on-camera scenes for young actors. However, most of the scenes I found were written for one child and one adult, not two kids or two teens. But adults don't attend acting classes for kids. Plus, I wanted my students to have the chance to portray characters their own age that they could relate to. This also helps prep them for real auditions, where they will only read for characters within their age range.

In addition to scene study and on-camera classes, many of my students participate in competitions and attend auditions where they need to present two-person scenes. In recent years, more directors have been open to seeing short scenes for auditions in place of monologues. In both the competitions and auditions, the scenes must be age-appropriate and free of costumes, props, and sound cues. The students primarily perform with partners of the same age and need material strong enough to get callbacks or win awards. Again, in my search for scenes, I found resources lacking.

Finally, after hearing the same problem voiced by fellow acting teachers, I decided to attempt to remedy the situation. Hence, the Winners' Competition Series scene books for kids and teens.

I started by writing scenes for the students I was teaching and putting them to the test: real auditions and competitions (not to mention, kid approval). The students fared well, receiving callbacks and awards. I decided to bring other writers onboard. As a writer, I have a particular style and tone, especially when it comes to comedy. I was getting sick of hearing my own voice, but more importantly, I thought it would be beneficial to include various voices and senses of humor.

Over the course of putting these books together, my colleagues and I found they served several purposes. Some of the acting teachers I know used the scenes for school talent shows or class performances. Other instructors used the scenes for national acting competitions. A nondrama teacher used them as a classroom activity just for fun. And I used the scenes during private coaching as cold-reading practice for my students' upcoming auditions. We all found the scenes valuable because, not only were they easy to memorize, practice, and present, the kids had a blast performing them. I strongly believe that children gain confidence and conquer fear of public speaking and performance when they are having fun. Additionally, young students

Acting class in Atlanta.

are more apt to pursue acting if they start out with enjoyable material.

So here I present you with the culmination of a lot of hard work and effort to provide you with the resources my colleagues and I once wished we could find. I want to thank the many wonderful writers and amazing students who contributed their talents and made these books possible.

I hope you find this new scene series to be as useful and valuable as I intended it to be. Whether you're a teacher, a parent, or an actor yourself, my wish is that you find exactly what you're looking for within these pages. So go ahead—dive in, test the waters, have fun! Just don't forget to breathe between giggles.

Best wishes and break a leg!

—Janet B. Milstein
www.janetmilstein.com

Tips on Using This Book and Choosing a Scene

When editing and organizing this book, I tried to make it as easy to use as possible. Here's what you should know:

- The scenes in this book are original and self-contained—they are not from plays.

- All the scenes are comedic.

- The scenes were written by numerous writers, exposing students to a variety of voices and helping them improve comedic tone and timing.

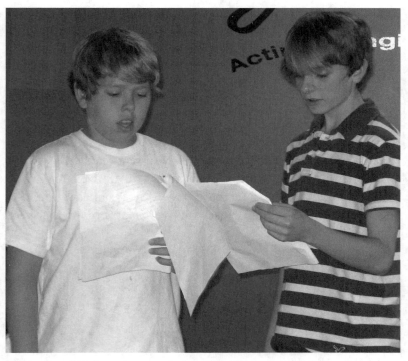

Hunter and Tyler rehearse their scene "Mesmerized."

- The scenes are ninety seconds and under—short enough for easy memorization and long enough to make a memorable impression.

- The scenes require no costumes, props, or sound cues, so they are easy to perform anywhere at any time.

- All the scenes are written for two characters.

- The scenes are broken down into gender combinations: two females, two males, and one male and one female.

- A brief description of the situation is included for each scene.

- The scenes are perfect for competitions, auditions, on-camera classes, and introductory comic scene work.

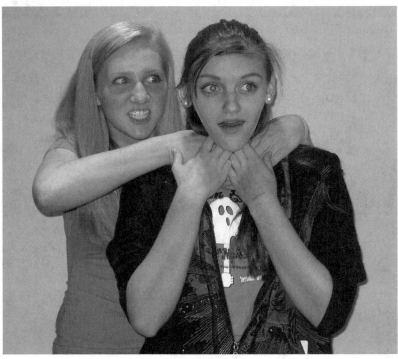

Jenna and Heather get seriously silly in their scene.

Ymi and Miguel perform a hilarious scene . . .

Sharing a kiss for the sake of comedy.

When choosing a scene, consider your age range and personality, the nature and language of the piece, and for what purpose you are using it. If a scene is being used for competitions or auditions, you should choose characters that are close to your age and type. Choosing a character that you could realistically be cast as will increase your auditioning success. If you are choosing a scene for class or a school project, often teachers will be more open to students playing characters older or younger than their actual ages. This will also give you the opportunity to explore different relationships and dynamics. If you are unsure about how important it is that the age of the character fits your age range, ask your acting teacher or coach.

Along the same lines, depending on what you are using the scene for, the nature and language of the scene you choose can be very important. You will find that the scenes in this book are free of foul language and that the circumstances are family-friendly. However, some teachers, directors, and judges at competitions will have their own idea of what is acceptable. Check any guidelines you are given, and when in doubt, ask your teacher or acting coach if the scene you chose is appropriate. If you find a word that might be offensive in an otherwise eligible scene, simply replace the word with something more suitable. Keep in mind, though, that the playwrights' words should be respected, and when learning your lines, you should not change or paraphrase the dialogue.

Because scenes, unlike monologues, are performed with partners, it is important that you work with your partner in choosing a scene. Whether your partner is assigned to you or someone you choose, you still want to come to an agreement about a scene you both would like to perform. Remember, a scene is a give-and-take between the actors, and deciding on a scene together is a good way to start the teamwork. When choosing a scene with your partner, pick a piece that excites you both—one that makes you laugh or think "I can totally relate to this!" Sometimes it's also fun to pick characters that are very different from you to explore life in their shoes. It is crucial that both of you like the scene you choose. If you don't have fun performing it, chances are your audience won't have fun watching it.

Sometimes, teachers prefer to assign scenes instead of letting partners choose their own. Actors need to adjust to the material they receive. If you do not like your scene, however, your teacher may be open to you bringing in an alternate scene. You might be surprised what a bit of enthusiasm or homework can do.

Pick your scene(s) far in advance of your upcoming audition or performance! It can sometimes take a bit of searching before you and your partner find a scene that you both really like. Also realize that choosing, rehearsing, and memorizing the scene all take time. If you wait until the last minute, you will not be adequately prepared.

You will see the word *beat* in parentheses *(Beat.)* in some of the scenes. A beat is a pause and is usually used to indicate that a character is thinking, hesitating, or waiting. Occasion-

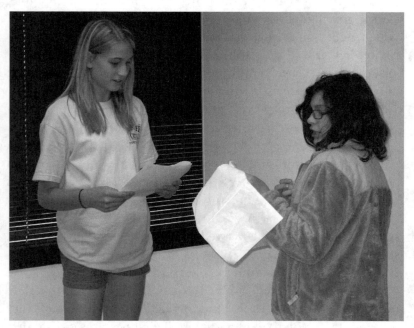

Running lines is an important part of scene study.

Nicholas and Joseph get silly while rehearsing their scene.

ally, a beat is included because an offstage "invisible" character is speaking. Beats are silent, but there is still a lot going on underneath the surface. Think of times in your life when someone gave you a look or you were afraid to say the wrong thing or you played eye-tag with your crush across the room. When you're taking a beat because an offstage character is speaking, you must figure out exactly what the person is saying. Choose specific lines or actions for that person and write them out on your scene. Do the same for yourself when your character is pausing—write out what you are thinking during each beat. Then, memorize what you wrote so you can run the lines in your head when you perform the scene. That way, you won't feel self-conscious or drop out of the scene during those silent moments. It is the actor's job to decide what is happening during each beat to keep those moments full and alive.

Scene Assignment

Answer the following questions for your scene/character very specifically so that you can *personalize* and relate to the situation and facts (the given circumstances). Look for clues in the text to help you make strong, applicable choices.

Four Things That Make a Good Goal

1. The goal you choose must be something you can only get through the other character. Bad example: *I want to be happy.* Good example: *I want David to ask me to go to the dance.*

2. Set your goal high—go for your dream! The higher you set your stakes, the harder you'll have to fight to get what you want, and the more exciting it will be for you and for the audience. *Test it*: If you get it, are you 100 percent satisfied? If not, go back and find a new goal that excites you.

3. Your goal must be achievable *now*! Otherwise, you have no chance of getting your goal. Bad example: *I want Brian to call me next week.* Good example: *I want Brian to ask for my number.* It's OK if a goal is unrealistic, such as, *I want Brian to ask me to marry him*—just as long as it is physically possible.

4. Your goal should not be based on the outcome of the scene. Often, characters don't get their goals. Instead, choose what you think your character truly wants. What is driving his or her behavior through the scene?

1. **Who?** Who is the *other person* in relation to your character? What is your relationship like? How close are you? Even if you are strangers, what is your first impression? Answer in as much detail as if you are speaking about someone from real life.

2. **What?** What is your character fighting for in the scene? Let's call this your *goal*. Your goal is what you, as your character, want to get from the other person/character. Your goal is not given to you. You need to pick a goal based on the script, your creativity, and what will personally make you connect with the scene.

3. **Where?** Where is this scene taking place? A classroom? In your backyard? Have you been here before? What's in the space? Is it bright, cluttered, noisy, peaceful, or creepy? How do you feel in the space? What is the best way to set up this scene so that you and your partner both can be easily seen and know where invisible objects are?

4. **When?** When is the scene taking place? What time period is it? What year is it? What season is it? What day of the week? What time of day? We feel very different at one in the morning versus one in the afternoon. What's the weather like? How does the time affect your mood?

Understanding Actions and Tactics

Actions, or tactics, are the things you do to the other character in an attempt to get your goal. When using tactics or actions, put them in the form "to [verb] the other person" (to bribe, to scare, to charm). You do this naturally in life. When you want your parents to buy you new jeans, what do you try to do? To guilt-trip them? To beg them? To please them? To irritate them?

---

5. **How?** How are you going to get your goal from the other person/character? By playing different *actions*, also known as *tactics*. Always write your actions in verb form (to beg, to scare, to delight). Write down some actions you might use to get your goal and then decide which lines would be a good place to try the different actions you picked. Watch your partner's reactions. If your tactic isn't working, change it to another one, such as from threaten to flatter. If it seems to be working, go further with it!

6. **Why?** Why do you want your goal? What is driving you? What will happen if you don't get it? For example, if your goal is to get your mom to let you use the computer, your "why" might be because you're dying to IM your best friend. Most of the time, there's a reason why we do the things we do, so it's very important to figure out why you want your goal and pick a strong reason that makes you want to get it right now This way you will *raise the stakes* and fight harder for your goal.

Creating the Moment Before

Your scene doesn't start with the first line. Your character has been going through a full day just like you. If the scene starts with her running up to her best friend after third period crying, it could be because her boyfriend just broke up with her in class. And her best friend also has something going on. She's not just standing at her locker. Perhaps she just got an F on her test, or she's worried about her hair, or she's trying to find her homework before the bell rings. Look for clues in the opening lines of the scene so that you make choices that are in line with your character's mood and behavior.

---

7. **The Moment Before**   What just happened the *moment before* the scene began? What was said or done? Where are you coming from? This is very important. Choose a specific event or situation that just happened to your character that will make you need to play out the scene right now! Test the situation you choose: Does it get you into the scene even before you speak your first line?

Scenes for Two Females

All in the Shake

by Lindsay Price

Sarah: 16 to 18 years old, female
Ginny: 16 to 18 years old, female

Sarah approaches her friend Ginny with bad news.

SARAH: Unbelievable!

GINNY: What?

SARAH: Unbelievable!

GINNY: What?

SARAH: I did *not* get the job. I didn't get the job!

GINNY: *(Turning away, perhaps a little guiltily.)* Sarah, I have something to tell you.

SARAH: *(Not listening.)* How could this happen? How could I have NOT got that JOB? I was perfect for it! The person who got the job could not have been more perfect than me.

GINNY: Funny you should say that, because I have something really funny to tell you about who might have got that—

SARAH: *(Interrupting.)* I followed my interview book to a T! My outfit was flawless. I presented a positive image. I had a firm but brief handshake. I spent weeks on that handshake!

GINNY: *(Shaking out her hand.)* I remember . . . lots of practice.

SARAH: What could have possibly gone wrong? Nothing went wrong!

GINNY: Well, and I'm only saying this as an outside chance, something to think about, maybe. Maybe, they were looking for more than a nice blouse and a good handshake.

SARAH: But that's what the book said. A firm handshake will always get you the job!

GINNY: Well, maybe, maybe, and I'm just throwing this out there, maybe they went with someone . . . *(She smiles and stands up straight.)* who really wanted the job, who can't believe she gets to work the whole summer at a TV station. Maybe one day she'll be a big name producer, sitting in the control room, running the show. *(She sighs.)*

SARAH: Sabotage.

GINNY: What?

SARAH: Someone didn't want me to get that job. That's what's going on here. Someone with a handshake like a cold fish and a wrinkled scoop necked blouse. This is out-and-out sabotage!

GINNY: No it's not! *(She coughs.)* I mean . . . who knows what they were thinking? But you know what? It's their loss. There'll be other jobs. Bigger jobs. Jobs that appreciate a strong, firm shake.

SARAH: Yeah . . . You're right. *(Throwing her arms around Ginny.)* Thank you, Ginny. You're the best friend a person could have. Now, what did you want to tell me?

GINNY: *(Backing away, talking fast.)* I got the job instead of you don't hate me, bye! *(She runs offstage.)*

SARAH: What? Liar! Traitor! Sabatoger! You stole my shake!

Almost Famous

by Monica Flory

Angela: 13 to 15 years old, female
Ella: 13 to 15 years old, female

Angela runs into Ella in the hallway at school.

ANGELA: You missed band practice yesterday.

ELLA: What?

ANGELA: We are never going to be a top-selling girl band if you don't come to practice.

ELLA: We'll never be a girl band, period. First of all, neither one of us play instruments.

ANGELA: Yes, we do! I play the harmonica. And the tambourine! And you sing!

ELLA: Badly. I sing badly.

ANGELA: Hey! No negativity! And what about the other girls? They play drums and bass.

ELLA: What other girls?

ANGELA: The ones we're going to ask to be part of our band!

ELLA: You're delusional.

ANGELA: I'm optimistic. You'll see when our debut album goes platinum.

ELLA: Album?! We don't even have a single song.

ANGELA: That's right! We have to do a single first and become a top iTunes download. Good thinking!

ELLA: Hello! Angela! We haven't even written any songs.

ANGELA: That's OK. The drummer writes songs.

ELLA: What drummer?

ANGELA: The one who's joining our band!

ELLA: Oh. Yeah. Right. Stupid me. What was I thinking? And the bass player? Does she write songs, too?

ANGELA: Don't be silly! She writes the lyrics!

ELLA: Of course she does!

ANGELA: See? Look how much we accomplished. Positivity is the key to success.

ELLA: And reality is the key you lost. Wake up, Angela! The drummer does not write songs! The drummer has left the building! And the lyric-writing bass player? She's bogus!

ANGELA: Oh my gosh—are you guys all fighting? Oh no! Does this mean the band is breaking up?

ELLA: That's one way of looking at it.

ANGELA: Well then, I better get started on our tell-all memoir.

The Date Escape

by Monica Flory

Bonnie: 16 to 18 years old, female
Erin: 16 to 18 years old, female

Erin walks into the restroom in a restaurant, where Bonnie is waiting.

BONNIE: I'm so glad you're here!

ERIN: Have we met?

BONNIE: No. But my mother always says that strangers are just friends you haven't met yet.

ERIN: Even people you meet in public restrooms?

BONNIE: Why not? A friend in need is an instant BFF.

ERIN: *(Trying to get past her to get into the stall.)* Excuse me, I've gotta go, if you know what I mean.

BONNIE: No! You have to help me.

ERIN: Help you what? You are standing way too close.

BONNIE: Sorry. *(Moves closer, blocking the stall.)* But you have to help me get out of this restaurant!

ERIN: OK . . . The doors you used to get in here? They work both ways. Now, if you'll kindly get out of my way . . .

BONNIE: I'm on the worst date of my life with the nicest guy who ever lived.

ERIN: And I'm supposed to . . .

BONNIE: Help me sneak out! If I go back to that table, I'll have to stay for the next two hours, because, he's just so nice, you know? He's the sweetest boy on earth.

ERIN: If he's so nice—

BONNIE: Because he's boring. So boring. I've had three cups of coffee just to stay awake while he talks. Please, for the love of sisterhood, help me get out of here!

ERIN: I'm sorry. I have to pee. And I'm on the best date of my life. I've only been away for a minute, and I miss him already. I mean, he's amazing—so smart and funny. And he looks like a younger Brad Pitt.

BONNIE: How nice for you! But can we please focus on the reason that we're here?

ERIN: I'd like to, if you would just move.

BONNIE: If there was a window in here, I could just hop out. There does seem to be a crawlspace—maybe you could hoist me up?!

ERIN: I spent three hours putting together this outfit. You think I'm gonna let you get footprints on it?

BONNIE: I'll take off my shoes!

ERIN: Leave the shoes on and back away.

BONNIE: OK. Maybe not. Are you opposed to yelling "fire" in a crowded restaurant? *(Erin gives her a look.)* Perhaps you'd like to distract my date by flirting with him?

ERIN: Oh yeah! Cause boring guy sounds so much better than my own Brad Pitt!

BONNIE: Point taken. Do you think I could sneak out unnoticed wrapped in toilet paper?

ERIN: OK, we are done. *(She starts to push her way to the bathroom stall.)* And if you're still here when I get out, I'm calling the cops.

BONNIE: Yes! That's a great idea! Thank you, sister! Dessert's on me. *(She exits happily.)*

Food Fight

by Elaine Tuman

Lisa: 14 to 16 years old, female
Rose: 14 to 16 years old, female

Lisa and Rose are in front of the principal, who is offstage. Lisa is a conformist, student-council type. Rose is an outsider, rebellious type.

LISA: Hello Principal Forsythe. Thanks for letting us tell our side of the story.

ROSE: It's an interesting story.

LISA: Yesterday, in the lunchroom, I invited . . .

ROSE: Summoned is more like it.

LISA: Rose to come sit with us.

ROSE: For an interrogation.

LISA: I just wanted to ask her some questions.

ROSE: It was like the Inquisition.

LISA: Ever hear of a friendly gesture?

ROSE: Ever hear of a setup?

LISA: We just don't understand Rose.

ROSE: The feeling's mutual.

LISA: We wondered why she draws skulls on her books and hangs out with boys with pink hair and rings in their noses. And if she must paint her nails black, she could at least get a manicure.

ROSE: I do bite my nails.

LISA: That's unsanitary.

ROSE: And a tension reliever.

LISA: So, anyway, it's not surprising—

ROSE: That tensions rose.

LISA: We got angry.

ROSE: Seriously angry. Even biting my nails didn't help.

LISA: She threw the first sandwich.

ROSE: Quite the sacrifice. It was a great sandwich. Tofu loaf, mayonnaise, Provolone cheese.

LISA: Right into my hair. It was disgusting.

ROSE: Mayonnaise is a great conditioner.

LISA: I hate to admit that we retaliated. We pelted her with carrot sticks.

ROSE: They're surprisingly lethal. I have a bruise.

LISA: At some point the rest of the cafeteria joined in.

ROSE: I guess that would make us the instigators.

LISA: Well, technically, Rose instigated the instigating.

ROSE: Brownnoser.

LISA: But we are truly sorry and regret our disgraceful behavior. So, Principal Forsythe, what I really want to know is . . .

ROSE: *(Hopeful.)* Was it videotaped?

LISA: *(Almost overlapping. Worried.)* Will this go on my permanent record?

Freedom

by Erin Austin

Melanie: 16 years old, female
Kate: 16 years old, female

Melanie and Kate sit side by side facing the audience. Melanie is driving, and Kate is in the passenger seat of the car.

MELANIE: Keys in the ignition. Check mirrors, seat belts, and we're good to go.

KATE: Omigosh, you're driving! We're going out by ourselves in your car! This is the coolest.

MELANIE: The coolest! I've been waiting for today for an entire year.

KATE: All that practice, with your parents in the front seat.

MELANIE: No more. I got the license and therefore I call the shots.

KATE: So where to?

MELANIE: I told my dad we're going to the mall.

KATE: So? It's the open road. You call the shots, remember? Besides, who wants to go to the mall?

MELANIE: We could go to the arcade!

KATE: The movies!

MELANIE: The beach!

KATE: Jason's house!

(They shriek with excitement.)

MELANIE: You're right. Forget the mall.

KATE: I'm calling Jason right now!

(Melanie looks into her rearview mirror.)

MELANIE: Uh-oh.

KATE: What?

MELANIE: Behind us.

(Kate turns around to look out the back window.)

MELANIE: Don't! He'll see!

(Kate quickly scrunches down into her seat.)

KATE: Your dad followed us?

MELANIE: Some first taste of independence.

KATE: Some freedom.

MELANIE: I can't believe he's tailing me.

KATE: And now he's pulling up beside us.

(The girls look over to the right and wave.)

MELANIE: So. How about we go to the mall?

KATE: I think the mall is exactly where I want to go right now.

MELANIE: Me too.

Get Your Cheer in Gear

by Diana Xin

Amy: 13 to 16 years old, female
Becky: 13 to 16 years old, female

Becky tries to convince her friend Amy to try out for the cheer-leading team with her.

AMY: Cheerleading? Really, Becky? I mean, cheerleading?

BECKY: Please, please, please, *pleeease*, Amy? Do it for me?

AMY: Why not tennis, or debate? Why does it have to be cheerleading?

BECKY: You don't have to join! It's just tryouts. They probably won't even pick you. You have very little cheer.

AMY: Exactly. So why should I try out?

BECKY: For me! Moral support! I'll look even peppier if you stand next to me. *(She does a few stretches.)* Come on, what do you have to lose?

AMY: Dignity? Self-respect? Postmodern gender studies book group?

BECKY: Postmodern . . . Ohhhh! Because John Hammerstein is in there.

AMY: What?! No! I am extremely fond of the study of gender.

BECKY: Mmm hmmm? I'm sure.

AMY: Look, I have a reputation to uphold. I can't be trying out for the bimbo team.

BECKY: Why not? I'll tell everyone you did it for me. That you're a great friend. A wonderful friend. The best friend in the world.

AMY: Your flattery's falling flat.

BECKY: Give me an A! Give me an M! Give me a Y! Gooooo Amy!

AMY: Give me an A-W-A-Y. Go away!

BECKY: Come on, Amy! You're my best friend. Are you really gonna make me face those mean, snobby, horrible cheerleaders alone?

AMY: Why do you want to be one if you know they're horrible?

BECKY: Because it looks fun. Come on!

AMY: Do I have to?

BECKY: Just picture it. We'll go to all the football games—

AMY: Kill me now.

BECKY: Everyone will want to be our friends.

AMY: Fake friends.

BECKY: *And* . . . boys. All boys like cheerleaders.

AMY: Not boys like John Hammerstein.

BECKY: Trust me. *All boys. (Beat.)* Will you do it?

AMY: OK. But you should know, I took four years of gymnastics!

Gnome-Caller

by Barbara Lhota and Janet B. Milstein

Tiffany: 15 to 18 years old, female
Precious: 15 to 18 years old, female

Tiffany approaches Precious at the lockers at school and folds her arms. Precious looks at Tiffany and puts her hands on her hips. They stare at each other. Tiffany tries to remain patient.

TIFFANY: Well?

PRECIOUS: Yeah?

TIFFANY: *(Beat, looks at her.)* Don't you have something to say to me?

PRECIOUS: Uh . . . me?! Christa said you were finally ready to apologize.

TIFFANY: What?! Why would *I* apologize to *you*? She said *you* were going to apologize to *me*!

PRECIOUS: Why would *I* apologize?! Everything that has gone down is *your* fault.

TIFFANY: My fault?! You're the one who had to flirt with Josh in biology and get us kicked out. Otherwise we never would've ditched school, stole the gnome, and caused the crossing-guard fiasco!

PRECIOUS: No, no, no! My flirting didn't get us kicked out. It was your *reacting* to my flirting—your bombastic snort that did us in! And by the way, whose idea was it to get a gnome-crossing-the-street-photo at high noon?!

TIFFANY: High noon?

PRECIOUS: Whatever!

TIFFANY: HELLO—you stole the gnome, you, you . . . gnome-a-nizer!

PRECIOUS: Snort-a-snitch!

TIFFANY: Overexert-a-flirt!

PRECIOUS: Gnome-offender-bender!

TIFFANY: Ditch-stigator! Cutting-class-a-fier!

PRECIOUS: *(Imitates Tiffany's typical pout.)* Model-lip-pout-a-poser!

TIFFANY: *(Gasps. Imitates Precious's typical hair twirl.)* Hair-twirl-a-twit!

PRECIOUS: Liar!

TIFFANY: Phony!

PRECIOUS/TIFFANY: *(Simultaneously.)* Rude!

TIFFANY: *(Pause.)* So we're made up?

PRECIOUS: Definitely.

TIFFANY: Cool.

PRECIOUS/TIFFANY: *(They wave cutely and walk off in opposite directions.)* Later!

Happily Ogre After

by Lindsay Price

Viola: 15 to 18 years old, female
Jane: 15 to 18 years old, female

Viola and Jane are preparing to cheat on an exam.

VIOLA: I can't believe we're doing this.

JANE: Say it.

VIOLA: Why?

JANE: Say it! Say it Vi.

VIOLA: I want an A.

JANE: Say it loud! Say it proud!

VIOLA: I want an A! Jane, this is stupid.

JANE: Will you get an A? Even if you study like your life depended on it?

VIOLA: No.

JANE: You will *not* get an A! Say it!

VIOLA: I will not get an A.

JANE: *Unless* you cheat.

VIOLA: I know, but—

JANE: *(Puts her hands up to silence her.)* Shhp! Say it.

VIOLA: Unless I cheat.

JANE: Exactly. So are you in, or are you out?

VIOLA: In. No, out. In. No! I'm out! Definitely out!

JANE: Viola!

VIOLA: What if we get caught? I can't bear it. I can't, I won't, I'll die!

JANE: Don't think like that. Negative thoughts! Negative energy! Boom—Negative results! Positive thoughts! Positive energy! Ding—Positive results!

VIOLA: That's bull. That's like saying people get cancer because they're pessimistic.

JANE: They do. And trust me. It's not fun.

VIOLA: Jane!

JANE: Hey! I don't make the rules.

VIOLA: There are no rules! We're cheating!

JANE: Look, are you in or out? Final answer.

VIOLA: You know, if you channeled this energy into your homework, you wouldn't have to cheat.

JANE: This is more fun. Let's review. Why do *you* need to cheat?

VIOLA: I . . . I want an A. And I'll never get it. I'll never go to college, I'll never get out of this backwoods town, and I'll wind up married to some dumb hairy ogre, cooking his moose and having baby ogres.

JANE: *(Beat. Looking digusted. Then happy.)* So you're in?

VIOLA: Yes. In. Definitely in.

JANE: Score!

VIOLA: So I'll sit next to Davis Dorkus and cheat off of him.

JANE: And I'll cheat off of you.

VIOLA: No way! This is my A! Get your own dorkus! Oh, and happily ogre after! *(Viola runs off.)*

JANE: *(Chasing after her.)* Uhhhh!

He's So . . . !

by John McGarvie

Ashley: 15 to 16 years old, female
Kara: 15 to 16 years old, female

Ashley and Kara are smitten with a boy in their class, until they learn something new about him.

ASHLEY: Omigod . . . Bradley is so cute!

KARA: Omigod . . . he's adorable!

ASHLEY: He's got like such cute dimples!

KARA: And his hair! I just want to run my fingers through it.

ASHLEY: I saw him jogging around the track . . . without his shirt!

KARA: *(Jumps up and down.)* OMIGOD!

ASHLEY: And he had on these blue shorts. They were so tight!

KARA: Omigod, Ashley!

ASHLEY: I thought I was gonna die! He's so gorgeous!

KARA: He sits across from me in chem lab.

ASHLEY: You are so totally lucky.

KARA: Wait . . . *(Using her hand as a phone.)* I'm getting a text from Michelle. *(Reads and gets a grossed-out look on her face.)* Eww! Michelle saw Bradley kissing Carol Stegman in the parking lot behind McDonald's yesterday!

ASHLEY: Yuck! He was kissing that loser?

KARA: Eww . . . they had their arms around each other.

ASHLEY: Ugh! She's so gross! What does he see in her?

KARA: Ash . . . Bradley's not so cute anymore.

ASHLEY: I know! Not if he's kissing *her*! He's so . . . ehhhh!!

(They shudder. They both stare out, depressed. Then their eyes focus on someone in front of them to the right and follow him across the stage to the left.)

ASHLEY: Omigod . . . Austin is so cute!

(Kara nods in eager agreement.)

I'll Die

by Elayne Heilveil

Kimmy: 13 to 15 years old, female
Karin: 13 to 15 years old, female, may wear glasses

Kimmy and Karin are on the sidelines at a party when they spot "Him."

KIMMY: Oh my God, he's walking towards us!

KARIN: *(Squints.)* Who?

KIMMY: Laugh!

(They laugh for effect, then stop.)

KIMMY: If he stops to talk, I'll die.

KARIN: Cheryl Turtlebaum's sister's best friend choked on a pickle.

(They laugh again. Abruptly stop.)

KIMMY: A pickle?

KARIN: In front of this guy. She was pretending to laugh at one of his jokes, and she was like sucking this pickle.

KIMMY: God, if I choked in front of Kevin . . . I would hope that I'd die.

KARIN: You mean *Kevin* Kevin?

KIMMY: *(Dreamily.)* With the ears. The itty bitty teeny baby ears.

KARIN: I know. They're so cute. I'm surprised he can hear.

KIMMY: *(Seriously.)* I smelled him.

KARIN: What?

KIMMY: I dropped my pencil, and when I leaned down to get it, I smelled him. And you know what he did? Paused.

KARIN: He didn't!

KIMMY: Uh-huh. He paused. And then . . . he breathed.

KARIN: No!

KIMMY: And then *I* breathed. And all of a sudden . . . it was as if we were breathing . . . as one! So I'm not going to breathe until he stops . . . and speaks . . . and breathes. Again. And if he does . . . I'll die!

KARIN: *(Spots him.)* Oh my God! It's *him.*

(They both have big frozen smiles as if he's coming toward them, then turn their heads as if he passed them by.)

KIMMY: *(Disappointed.)* I guess I won't die after all.

KARIN: I could get you a pickle.

Killer Cookie

by Lindsay Price

Shauna: 14 to 16 years old, female
Anne: 14 to 16 years old, female, a bad cook

Anne gets a taste of Anne's unique new method of impressing a boy.

SHAUNA: *(She grabs her throat.)* Agh! *(She grabs her stomach and groans.)* Oooh!

ANNE: It's not that bad.

SHAUNA: *(She collapses to the floor.)* Ugh!

ANNE: It can't be that bad.

SHAUNA: That was the worst cookie I ever ate in my whole entire life.

ANNE: It's really that bad?

SHAUNA: *(Getting up.)* First there was a rush of awful. Then a wave of horrific. And then I was choked in a sea of total yuck.

ANNE: Oh. That sounds pretty bad.

SHAUNA: That is the cookie of certain death. Killer cookie. Why would you make something so horrible? Why would you do that? Why?

ANNE: To impress Billy Smith.

SHAUNA: By killing him? *(Feels around her mouth.)* Uhh, I think I broke a tooth.

ANNE: I put my heart and soul into that cookie. I put care and tenderness. Any girl can flick her hair and giggle and make googly eyes at a boy. Any girl.

SHAUNA: Boys like it when girls do that.

ANNE: I am *not* any girl. I am Anne. I am unique. I want Billy to look at me and see *me*, not hair and giggles and bulging pupils. I want Billy to look at me and say, "No one has ever made cookies for me before. You are special, Anne Bowman. I love you. I will always love you."

SHAUNA: Maybe you should skip the garlic.

ANNE: But garlic is good for your heart.

SHAUNA: I think Billy's heart can fend for itself.

ANNE: No it can't! It's under attack. There are a gazillion girls around Billy every day flicking and giggling and googling. I need to stand out! I need to be unique!

SHAUNA: Unique, yes. Fatal, no!

ANNE: Shauna! What am I going to do?

SHAUNA: *(Grabbing Anne by the shoulders.)* Anne! My mom is an awesome baker. She'll help you make killer cookies. The right kind. Not the dead kind.

ANNE: Really?

SHAUNA: Come on.

(They start to exit.)

ANNE: I guess I should go throw the cookies away.

SHAUNA: No, leave them. They'll make a great gift for Principal Jackson!

Lucky Sock

by Lindsay Price

Deanne: 15 to 16 years old, female
Missy: 15 to 16 years old, female

Deanne loses one of her lucky socks, and it may not have been an accident. Missy chases Deanne onstage.

DEANNE: Look. I'll just wear one. It's no big deal.

MISSY: No big deal?!

DEANNE: It'll be my thing. My trick. The girl who wears one sock. It's no big deal.

MISSY: Deanne. Were you, or were you not, wearing your lucky socks when you hit that homerun in the ninth inning? Were you, or were you not, wearing your lucky socks when Trent Toller finally noticed your existence?! Tonight's game is our shot at the championship! I am not going to lose because you lost that sock!

DEANNE: I get it! I get it! But I can't . . . get it! My dryer ate the sock, and it won't give it back. But, it's OK! Because I've still got the one!

MISSY: Luck doesn't work in the odd, Deanne. Luck only works in pairs! Unlucky thirteen. Lucky four-leaf clover! Two not one!

DEANNE: Don't you think I know that? I know that! What am I supposed to do?

MISSY: The only thing to do. You have to confront your dryer.

DEANNE: *(She gasps in horror.)* What? I can't!

MISSY: You have to get the sock back. We need that pair of lucky socks. Uneven luck is bad.

DEANNE: You don't know my dryer. This is not about socks. This is bigger than socks. My dryer is very temperamental. Use the wrong fabric softener, and she won't dry things for weeks. You don't understand.

MISSY: What are you saying? *(She gasps, and her eyes go wide.)* The dryer took your lucky sock on purpose? Like a punishment or something?

DEANNE: *(Whispering.)* I think so. She knew it was my lucky sock, and she ate it! She's trying to throw off my luck! I'm terrified to go anywhere near the basement.

MISSY: But we need that sock! *(She stops and turns to Deanne, her eyes narrowing.)* What did you do to get your dryer so mad at you? Did you mix darks and lights? What?

DEANNE: Oh . . . it was nothing. I thought it was nothing. It was a harmless offhanded remark!

MISSY: Dryers don't punish without reason. You're not telling the whole story. Spill!

DEANNE: I may have . . . said I . . . love having my clothes dry-cleaned. *(She winces.)*

MISSY: *(Gasping.)* Idiot!

DEANNE: I know! I didn't mean it! I'm sorry.

MISSY: Don't apologize to me. You need to beg your dryer. *(She falls to her knees and clasps her hands in front of her chest.)* Please Ms. Dryer. I didn't mean it! I'll never disrespect you again!

DEANNE: Do you think it'll work?

MISSY: We can only hope, Deanne. We can only hope. Cross your lucky sock.

(They run offstage.)

MySpace

by Janet B. Milstein

Elizabeth: 13 to 16 years old, female
Lexy: 13 to 16 years old, female

Elizabeth and Lexy went on Elizabeth's dad's computer without permission, and it just crashed.

ELIZABETH: *(Briskly enters and starts pacing.)* Oh my God. Oh my God. What are we gonna do?

LEXY: Relax.

ELIZABETH: That's easy for you to say!

LEXY: It's easy for you too. Try it. *(Overarticulates as if teaching her to speak.)* Reelaax.

ELIZABETH: Lexy!

LEXY: Or not.

ELIZABETH: This is serious. When my dad sees his computer we are so dead!

LEXY: We? He's *your* dad. It's *his* computer. I'm just visiting.

ELIZABETH: What?! This is all *your* fault!

LEXY: My fault? How is this my fault?

ELIZABETH: *(Mocking her.)* Let's go on MySpace. I wanna go on MySpace. I need to check my MySpace.

LEXY: Hey, it's not my fault his ancient computer couldn't handle my MySpace page.

ELIZABETH: The city of Chicago couldn't power your My-Space page. If it wasn't so attention seeking and show-offy, my dad's computer wouldn't have crashed.

LEXY: It didn't crash, it just sort of froze. It's not broken, it's in shock, that's all. And my MySpace is not show-offy. It's outgoing.

ELIZABETH: Yeah, like a cannonball!

LEXY: You're just jealous because it's so easy for me to make friends.

ELIZABETH: I'm not jealous.

LEXY: Yes you are.

ELIZABETH: No I'm not.

LEXY: Are too!

ELIZABETH: Am not! *(Beat. They stare each other down. Elizabeth gives in.)* OK, I am. But only because you talk to people so easily.

LEXY: Elizabeth, you do too.

ELIZABETH: Not like you.

LEXY: Well, yeah. I guess it's a gift. But I can teach you.

ELIZABETH: I don't know.

LEXY: Come on, I won't let you look bad. I promise.

ELIZABETH: Well . . . OK.

LEXY: Cool. So whoever you want to talk to, just let me know, and I'll start the conversation, and you just follow my lead.

ELIZABETH: OK. Let's start with my dad.

One Stupid Moment

by David-Matthew Barnes

Stacey: 13 to 15 years old, female
Rachel: 13 to 15 years old, female

Stacey is mortified after accidentally burping in front of a boy she likes. Her best friend, Rachel, tries to comfort her.

STACEY: I'm changing my name and moving to another country.

RACHEL: Stacey, you're totally overreacting.

STACEY: I completely burped right in his face.

RACHEL: I don't want to make you feel bad, but it was really loud, too.

STACEY: Do you think they heard me in the art room?

RACHEL: Yeah, and probably in the cafeteria, too.

STACEY: Are you serious?

RACHEL: Yeah, it echoed down the hallway.

STACEY: It *echoed*?! I am such a loser.

RACHEL: I thought it was kind of funny. Even Josh was laughing.

STACEY: No, he was crying because my tsunami burp blasted him into the lockers. I think he has a concussion.

RACHEL: Look on the bright side.

STACEY: Is there one?

RACHEL: I'm sure you made a lasting impression. He'll definitely remember you now.

STACEY: I'm transferring to another school tomorrow. *(Beat. She paces.)* Do you think maybe he'll just forget this ever happened?

RACHEL: He might . . . but the rest of the school won't.

STACEY: What do you mean?

RACHEL: Dana recorded the entire thing on her cell phone. You're probably being downloaded on the Internet as we speak.

STACEY: Come on. We're leaving.

RACHEL: Where are we going?

STACEY: Mexico.

(They exit quickly.)

Party Panic

by Janet B. Milstein

Kathryn: 16 to 18 years old, female
Haley: 16 to 18 years old, female

Kathryn is throwing a party at her house while her parents are away. She just got off the phone with them and needs help from her friend Haley.

KATHRYN: Oh my God, Haley!

HALEY: Hey, Kathryn! Great party! Jason Reed is here!

KATHRYN: Haley! You've got to help me!

HALEY: No way! He's mine!

KATHRYN: No, not him! My parents just called! They're coming home tonight! Not tomorrow. Now!

HALEY: *(Beat. Then laughs.)* You almost had me.

KATHRYN: I'm serious! I'm very serious! I'm dead serious! This party is over! We've got to get rid of everyone fast!

HALEY: How? There are tons of people here. I can't believe the turnout! I don't even know the people hanging in your parents' room.

KATHRYN: There are strangers in my parents' room? Great! Wonderful! I'm dead! What are they doing in there?

HALEY: I'm not sure. It was hard to see through all the smoke, but I think—

KATHRYN: Smoke?!

HALEY: Yeah, but I think I saw them passing your dad's stuffed sailfish through the fog.

KATHRYN: His sailfish?! That thing's bigger than me! How'd they get it off the wall?

HALEY: *(Shrugs.)* Where there's a will . . .

KATHRYN: *(Beat.)* I'm leaving town.

HALEY: Kathryn, chill out. We'll just hang it back up when they're done . . . doing . . . whatever they're doing. It'll be fine.

KATHRYN: Easy for you to say! You don't have rowdy people invading your house and doing . . . bizarre . . . things to your dad's favorite fish!

HALEY: They weren't rowdy.

KATHRYN: Haley! I need a plan to get them out right this minute!

HALEY: OK. *(Thinks.)* We could say we're out of beer!

KATHRYN: We did run out of beer! They just bought more!

HALEY: Oh, that was nice of them. *(Off Kathryn's look.)* OK, we could call the cops to kick them out.

KATHRYN: Yes! That's it! Because I always wanted a criminal record!

HALEY: Criminal records are totally in. Oh, hey, did you notice Jason's haircut? My God. He looks so hot!

KATHRYN: Hot? Hot?! *(Beat. Realizing.)* That's it! Go open my parents' bedroom door. Wide.

HALEY: What for?

KATHRYN: *(Yells.)* FIRE!!!

Sexy Funk

by Janet B. Milstein

Amy: 13 to 16 years old, female
Melissa: 13 to 16 years old, female

Amy sees her friend Melissa in the hall at school and approaches her.

AMY: *(Approaching.)* Hey, Melissa! I was looking for you. How did you . . . *(Reacts.)* What is that smell?

MELISSA: *(Excited.)* Which smell would that be?

AMY: The one that's terrorizing my nasal passages. *(She checks the bottom of her shoes.)*

MELISSA: *(Excited, fishing for a compliment.)* No seriously. What does it smell like?

AMY: Like you should seriously check your shoes! Where is that coming from? *(She sniffs around.)* Oh God—it's you! You stink!

MELISSA: I do not! I smell amazing!

AMY: Amazingly stinky! What is that foul odor?

MELISSA: It's not foul! It's a special aphrodisiacal spray. It's supposed to totally attract guys.

AMY: Are you sure it said guys, not flies?

MELISSA: Ha, ha.

AMY: What's it called?

MELISSA: Sexy Funk.

AMY: Well, they got the funk part right.

MELISSA: Oh, yeah? Well, Steven said I smell good today.

AMY: Steven Reynolds? *(Melissa nods.)* He's a total mouth breather!

MELISSA: Nuh-uh!

AMY: Have you ever seen him with his mouth closed?

MELISSA: *(Beat. She thinks, realizing Amy is right.)* Anyway . . . Kevin Harris said I look hot today.

AMY: He says that every day. To every girl!

MELISSA: You're just jealous!

AMY: No I'm not. Trust me. You smell like skunk funk.

MELISSA: Well, if you're so offended by my scent, why don't you go hang out somewhere else?!

AMY: Melissa, come on. I still like you, just not your . . . fumes. I'm just telling you, as your friend, go shower immediately. And then get a refund on that stuff. It obviously doesn't work at all.

MELISSA: Oh yeah? I guess that's why Andy Bradley asked me out this morning.

AMY: Andy Bradley? *(Melissa nods.)* Hand over that funk!

Solve for X

by Justin Warner

Paige: 14 to 18 years old, female
Liz: 14 to 18 years old, female

Paige and Liz sit next to each other in math. They have just finished a math test.

PAIGE: Hey, Liz, wait up!

LIZ: *(Surprised to see her.)* Paige. You're done too?

PAIGE: What did you think of the test? Pretty easy, huh?

LIZ: I think I bombed it.

PAIGE: *(Laughs.)* Yeah, right! Like you've ever bombed a test in your life.

LIZ: I'm serious. I was so busy working on my English paper that I totally forgot about the math test until eleven o'clock last night. And I stink at trigonometry.

PAIGE: *(Becoming concerned.)* But you finished so fast . . .

LIZ: I just wanted to get it over with. *(Realizing something.)* Oh, man!

PAIGE: *(More worried.)* What?

LIZ: Cosine is *adjacent* over hypotenuse!

PAIGE: Well, yeah . . . So?

LIZ: So, I got sine and cosine mixed up through the whole test.

PAIGE: No! I don't believe this! I *knew* it was adjacent but then you . . .

LIZ: But then I what?

PAIGE: Nothing.

LIZ: Were you copying off me?

PAIGE: Well, duh! You're only the smartest person in the whole school except for today!

LIZ: *(Suddenly triumphant.)* Yes!

PAIGE: What are you so happy about?

LIZ: I'm so sick of people copying off me all the time! When people find out you copied off me and failed, they'll finally leave me alone! *(She hugs Paige.)* Thank you! This F is going to be so totally worth it!

PAIGE: *(Disgusted.)* Whoopee.

Switch

by Dan Collins

Hannah: 13 years old, female
Emily: 13 years old, female

Hannah and Emily are twins and have just returned home from school after switching places for the day.

HANNAH: Did anyone notice?

EMILY: Why do you have to be such a loud mouth? Everyone kept asking why I was being so quiet.

HANNAH: Emily! You were supposed to act like me! That's part of switching places. Just because we're twins doesn't mean that no one's gonna notice. You've got to play the part!

EMILY: Well . . . were you quiet and shy?

HANNAH: Um . . . mostly.

EMILY: What do you mean mostly?

HANNAH: You're going to the spring dance with Ryan Oliver.

EMILY: What?!

HANNAH: He's so cute! And I don't have any classes with him, so I started talking to him and . . . well . . . I said I'd be his date.

EMILY: No, you said *I'd* be his date.

HANNAH: Well . . . yeah, but you don't want to go with him. I'll just go to the dance as you.

EMILY: No way, I'm going.

HANNAH: But he asked me.

EMILY: No, he asked me!

HANNAH: He asked the loudmouth, outgoing, funny version of you—which is me.

EMILY: Oh well.

HANNAH: Em! I had to work really hard to get him to ask me. I had to get a seat next to him, then strike up a conversation and make all the right jokes and laugh at all the right times *and* look cute while I was wearing your clothes— I earned that date!

EMILY: Listen, we did this stupid switch for you. I had to take your math test, my feet are killing me from wearing your shoes, I played competitive sports in gym with your girly girlfriends, *and* I risked my perfect attendance record. *I* earned this date.

HANNAH: But . . . it's Ryan Oliver.

EMILY: I know!

HANNAH: You better have aced that test!

(*Emily gives Hannah a big hug.*)

A Total Eugene

by Lindsay Price

Sue: 15 to 16 years old, female
Lisa: 15 to 16 years old, female

Best friends Lisa and Sue discuss Lisa's boyfriend and whether or not he's "right" for Lisa.

SUE: *(Comes running in.)* Lisa, we have to talk.

LISA: *(Looking at herself in the mirror.)* Do you like this top?

SUE: It's nice.

LISA: Eugene loves when I wear bright colors.

SUE: *(She makes a face and a noise.)* Eck! *(She composes herself.)* We have to talk.

LISA: Sure. *(Turning back to the mirror.)* What about?

SUE: About . . . about . . . *(She can't spit it out.)*

LISA: *(Fussing with her hair.)* Is my hair OK?

SUE: You have to break up with him!

LISA: Who?

SUE: Him!

LISA: Who him? *(She gasps.)* Eugene?

SUE: *(She makes a face and a noise.)* Gah! Yes!

LISA: *(She puts her hands on her hips.)* Why?

SUE: Lisa. *(She takes a deep breath and talks fast.)* You have a reputation. You have nice hair. You have friends. A lot of friends. Are you going to give all that up for, for—

LISA: Eugene?

SUE: Stop saying his name! The Lisas of this world can't go out with the Eugenes! Eugene. He's such a total . . . Eugene. His hair is Eugene. His glasses are Eugene. His message tees are Eugene. Nobody who is not cute should wear a message tee. Especially Eugene! You see?

LISA: I see. Oh boy, do I see.

SUE: Oh good. So you'll break up with him?

LISA: Oh no. Never. Eugene and his message tees are here to stay.

SUE: Lisa! You can't! You'd pick him over me?

LISA: You bet. You know what, Sue? You need a Eugene.

SUE: *(A look of horror.)* What? Why do I need a Eugene?

LISA: Trust me, you do. You think Eugene is bad because you've never dated anyone like him. You've only dated the Scotts and the Jordans and the Blakes of the world. Well, let me tell you something, Eugenes call you back. Eugenes don't stand you up. Eugenes . . . Eugenes listen when you talk! *(She claps her hands together.)* I should introduce you to one of his friends!

SUE: No! No Eugenes! *(She runs off.)*

LISA: *(Calling after her.)* I can introduce you to a Bernard! Or how about a Sherman? You'd love Sherm!

Totally Weird

by Karen Jeynes

Suzie: 13 to 16 years old, female
Lacey: 13 to 16 years old, female

Two ditzy blonde cheerleader types are chatting at lunch break. This is (obviously) a parody. Suzie is ever so slightly cooler than Lacey.

SUZIE: Hey, so the weirdest thing just happened!

LACEY: Tell! Tell!

SUZIE: I walked past Mark, and he totally looked at me!

LACEY: No!

SUZIE: Yes!

LACEY: No!

SUZIE: Totally!

LACEY: But he and Stacey—

SUZIE: Yes!

LACEY: Are they still—

SUZIE: Yes!

LACEY: Weird.

SUZIE: Totally weird.

LACEY: Did he look look or just look?

SUZIE: He look looked!

LACEY: Wow. *(Noticing someone.)* Oh, my word!

SUZIE: What?

LACEY: Dave is totally looking at you!

SUZIE: No way!

LACEY: Way!

SUZIE: No way!

LACEY: Way! I bet you're glad you didn't take it any further with Mark now, aren't you?

SUZIE: Totally. I mean, Dave is way hotter than Mark—

LACEY: Way!

SUZIE: Wait—did he look look or did he just look?

LACEY: He look looked.

SUZIE: Wow.

LACEY: Don't look, he's totally walking over!

(Silence. Both girls look in the same direction and pull cheesy smiles.)

SUZIE/LACEY: Hi!

SUZIE: Oh, my word, he totally said hi!

LACEY: I know!

SUZIE: I am so totally in love!

Scenes for Two Males

Caring Older Brother

by Matt Fotis

Blake: 13 to 14 years old, male, brother to Jeremy
Jeremy: 15 to 16 years old, male, brother to Blake

Blake just broke his mother's antique lamp. Luckily, his older brother, Jeremy, has a solution.

BLAKE: Oh, man, Mom is going to kill us.

JEREMY: She's going to kill *you*. I was being studious and doing my homework.

BLAKE: Spell *studious*.

JEREMY: Me spelling *studious* isn't going to fix Mom's lamp. That Grandma gave her. Right before she died.

BLAKE: I'm dead.

JEREMY: OK, since you're my brother, and I'm a caring, kind, and considerate person, here's what I'm going to do: First, you go to the store and buy some Super Glue and the new Zelda for Gameboy.

BLAKE: I don't have any money, Jeremy. And what's the Zelda for?

JEREMY: No time for trivial details, Blake! Do you want my help or not?

BLAKE: Right, sorry. Super Glue and Zelda. OK?

JEREMY: Second, you pay me a weekly fee of ten dollars.

BLAKE: What? Why? I'm not paying you—

JEREMY: Blake, Blake, Blake. You don't want me to tell Mom that you were throwing a football around *in the living room* and broke her lamp, do you?

BLAKE: OK, five dollars.

JEREMY: That she got from Grandma. Right before—

BLAKE: OK, fine, ten. I'm gonna have to get a job.

JEREMY: You do my laundry, mow the grass for the entire summer, and make my bed, and I'll reduce your fee to five bucks.

BLAKE: You're a horrible person. I want you to know that.

JEREMY: Do you want me to up it to twenty? Because, frankly, you're not in a position to negotiate, Blake. I'm cutting you a deal here.

BLAKE: I'm your brother, Jeremy. Flesh and blood.

JEREMY: Gosh, remember how mad Mom got when you came home with a hole in your jeans? She grounded you for a week. I wonder what she'll do to you now. After you broke her lamp. That she got from Gran—

BLAKE: How do you sleep at night?

JEREMY: Well, thanks. Now you better get going. Mom'll be home in an hour, and I'd hate to break the bad news.

BLAKE: You have no soul.

(Blake slowly sulks out.)

JEREMY: Bring me back a Snickers! *(To himself.)* Oh, that's right, Grandma gave Mom two matching lamps. You could get the other lamp out of the attic. Already gone, Blake? Shucks. So lucky to have a caring older brother.

Collateral

by Janet B. Milstein

Sean: 16 years old, male, brother to David
David: 13 to 15 years old, male, brother to Sean

David enters angrily, followed by Sean, and heads across the stage to exit, but Sean quickly runs in front of him, blocking his way.

SEAN: David, come on.
>   *(David angrily turns his back to Sean and says nothing. Sean crosses to face him.)*

SEAN: I said I was sorry.
>   *(Again David turns his back to Sean and says nothing. Sean crosses to face him.)*

SEAN: You're making a big deal out of nothing.

DAVID: Nothing? You left me at the gas station as collateral!

SEAN: I had to do something.

DAVID: I'm your brother. And you just handed me over to them like a stray dog.

SEAN: I was coming back.

DAVID: I could have been murdered by then.

SEAN: They weren't gonna do anything.

DAVID: How do you know? After you drove off, they stared at me and whispered about who would get each of my limbs!

SEAN: Don't be so dramatic.

DAVID: Me? What about you? Who goes to a gas station and says "fill her up" with no money?

SEAN: I've only had my license for two weeks. Gimme a break. I forgot. Usually Mom and Dad pay when we go to a gas station.

DAVID: True, but usually, when they do that, they're in the car!

SEAN: OK, so what was I supposed to do? I had to make them believe I'd come back with the money.

DAVID: So you give them your iPod or your license, not your brother!

SEAN: Chill out! You're home, you're fine, you're scar-free.

DAVID: Only on the outside. *(Gives Sean a serious look.)* You have no idea what I went through.

SEAN: You? What about me? Being a new driver is stressful enough, and I had to go find the money. I was hurrying back and even flattened one of Mr. Kessler's lawn gnomes.

DAVID: *(Smiling in spite of himself.)* I've always hated those gnomes. So where'd you get the money?

SEAN: Well, Mom wasn't home so I, sort of . . .

DAVID: Do not tell me you took the money I've been saving up!

SEAN: OK. I won't tell you.

DAVID: You disgust me. There is no way we are related. *(David turns and starts to leave.)*

SEAN: Where are you going?

DAVID: Back to the gas station. Those murderers treated me better than you.

The Higher Five

by Adam Simon

Jason: 16 to 18 years old, male
Trent: 16 to 18 years old, male

Jason and Trent walk toward each other in the hall.

JASON: Yo!
> *(Jason holds up his hand for a high five. Trent just stares at him.)*
JASON: Kinda leaving me hanging here, broseph.
TRENT: I'm sorry. I'm over the high five. I just can't fake it anymore.
JASON: You're "over" it?
TRENT: It just feels outdated to me.
JASON: Are you kidding me? This is going to be a big problem for me. I'm from a high-fiving family.
TRENT: What does that mean?
JASON: We prefer it to hugging . . . or, you know, talking. Look, if you're not gonna high five, what about this chestnut?
> *(Jason puts out his fist for a fist bump.)*
TRENT: I hate to say it—
JASON: No way!
TRENT: There's just got to be something better.
JASON: Nothing is better! There is nothing better than a high five. It's life affirming! Would you rather we chest bump?

TRENT: Well, I'm not—

(Jason gives him a rough chest bump.)

TRENT: Ow! I didn't say—

JASON: Bet you wish you had just high fived me now.

TRENT: I think you cracked my rib.

JASON: Innovation is rarely painless.

TRENT: What about this?

(Trent puts his hand out for a handshake.)

JASON: "The grandpa"? Seriously? Dude, I'd rather talk!

The Hitchhikers

by Edith Weiss

Dan: 13 to 16 years old, male
Mike: 13 to 16 years old, male

Dan and Mike walk onstage.

DAN: I am so tired of walking.

MIKE: We'll be there in fifteen minutes.

DAN: I'm cold.

MIKE: So let's run.

DAN: Let's hitchhike.

MIKE: Are you crazy? That's dangerous.

DAN: We're two guys. Come on, what could happen?

MIKE: Anything! Everything! Anything and everything could happen!

DAN: *(Sticks out thumb.)* I'm doing it. Are you with me?

MIKE: No! This is nuts!

DAN: Then I'll do it alone.

MIKE: OK, I'll do it. I'm not gonna let you hitchhike by yourself.

DAN: That car's slowing down!

(Mike, behind Dan, waves the car away. Dan doesn't see this.)

MIKE: Darn it. They changed their mind.

(A car slows down, then speeds up. Both do a semiturn, Dan with his thumb out, Mike waving them on but being careful not to let Dan see.)

DAN: What is going on?

MIKE: They're probably just slowing down to see if we're worth robbing.

DAN: Don't you have any faith in human nature?

MIKE: Not so much. We could have walked halfway there by now, you know?

(A car passes. They do the semiturn. This time Dan sees what Mike is doing.)

DAN: Mike! You're waving them on! That's why they're not stopping—they think we're crazy, hitchhiking and waving them on at the same time!

MIKE: We *are* crazy. This is crazy and it's dangerous!

DAN: You're just scared.

MIKE: I am not scared!

DAN: This car is slowing down.

(This time, with Dan watching, Mike doesn't wave the car on.)

MIKE: It's got a dead deer on the hood.

DAN: So?

MIKE: So they've got guns. Guns, Dan, that's all I'm saying.

DAN: Oh geez. Someone just threw a beer can out the window.

MIKE: Guns and beer. And dead deer. And they're stopping. Perfect!

DAN: I thought you weren't scared?

MIKE: I lied.

DAN: Me too!

DAN/MIKE: Runnnn!

(They run offstage.)

Inside Man

by Matt Van Tassel

Rob: 15 to 16 years old, male
Sam: 15 to 16 years old, male

Rob and Sam talk in the hallway after school.

ROB: Hey, Sam, you know what today is?

SAM: Thursday.

ROB: No dude.

SAM: Yeah it is.

ROB: No dude, today is exactly two weeks until I get my license.

SAM: Assuming you pass the test.

ROB: Don't worry about that. I might as well take the test on a deposit slip, because it's *money in the bank*!

SAM: That was lame. What makes you so sure you're going to pass?

(Rob looks around suspiciously.)

ROB: What if I were to tell you I have found the Rosetta stone of the Department of Motor Vehicles?

SAM: I don't even know what that means.

ROB: What if I were to tell you I have a certain inside man, through a certain academic assembly, who has access to all the answers to a certain test?

SAM: Then I would say you bought the driving manual from that guy Joon-Kim who you sit next to in algebra.

ROB: What? How did you know that?

SAM: Because he tried to sell it to me.

ROB: And you didn't buy it?!

SAM: No, I already have one. The DMV hands them out for free.

ROB: What? Are you serious? That double-crossing snake!

SAM: I can't believe you paid five bucks for that. You could have borrowed mine for free.

ROB: I can't believe it either. I bought it for twenty.

Jambalaya's Jalopies

by Lindsay Price

Pete: 16 years old, male
Byron: 16 years old, male

Pete is excitedly showing his friend Byron his first car (staged with two chairs). Byron is less than impressed.

PETE: So? What do you think?

BYRON: Is that duct tape?

PETE: The bumper's a little wobbly. But isn't it great?

BYRON: Is it certified?

PETE: I love it, man. I got a car! My first car!

BYRON: Pete, you should've had me come with you.

PETE: I didn't need you to come with me.

BYRON: Says the guy with the duct-tape car.

PETE: The car is fine.

BYRON: The car is a lemon. Who sold it to you?

PETE: Jambalaya.

BYRON: Jambalaya? You actually went to Jambalaya's Jalopies? No wonder it's a piece of junk!

PETE: Dude, it's totally fine! Jambalaya was fine, I'm fine, the car is fine.

BYRON: Pete, you can't tell what's rust and what's paint!

PETE: It adds character. Can't you just be happy for me? I wanted a car, I worked two jobs and I went and did this all by myself. Stop being my dad. I already have one.

BYRON: OK, OK, sorry. Can we go for a ride?

PETE: Sure! OK, when we get in, you have to bounce up and down before I start it.

BYRON: Bounce? Up and down?

(Pete sits down in the driver's seat, and Byron sits down in the passenger's seat.)

PETE: Jambalaya says that will help the gas flow properly. And lean to the left while you bounce.

BYRON: Lean and bounce?

PETE: Never mind. I'll lean and bounce. You get out and push.

Kissing 101

by Barbara Lhota

Sam: 13 years old, male
Aaron: 13 years old, male

Sam and Aaron stand in the library. They try to be quiet as they have a very important talk.

SAM: So here's the thing. I just want to, well, ya know, *(Looks around, whispers.)* kiss her.

AARON: Uh-huh.

SAM: But, see, I—

AARON: Need some help on technique? You came to the right library, Sam.

SAM: So you actually have experience at this? With who?

AARON: *(Whispers.)* Louise Halloren.

SAM: Full-frontal-dental-retainer Louise Halloren?!

AARON: Shh! Sister Rita. Two o'clock.

(They smile nervously as their eyes follow the offstage Sister Rita walking by.)

SAM: Louise? Disgusting. How can she kiss with that thing?

AARON: You'd be surprised. Besides, it's more experience than you have.

SAM: True. So, what's the technique?

AARON: Ten bucks.

SAM: Ten bucks! But I'm your best friend!

AARON: That's why I gave you the discount. Don't worry. Pay me tomorrow. Now, first, put your feet about five inches apart.

SAM: My feet? What do my feet have to do with kissing?

AARON: Stability. It's like golf or basketball. You need the proper stance.

SAM: Really? *(He puts his feet five inches apart.)* Is this OK?

AARON: Good. Now close your eyes.

SAM: *(Closes his eyes. Peeking.)* How will I know if she likes it if my eyes are closed?

AARON: Believe me, you don't wanna open your eyes. All you'll see is her nose all squished up close and big. Now open your mouth.

SAM: Here? In the school library?

AARON: You wanna dive in without practice? Open your mouth! *(Sam opens his mouth wide.)* Not like that! You aren't swallowing her head. *(Sam closes his mouth a bit.)* Now lean in.

SAM: *(He closes his eyes and leans in.)* I had no idea how much coordination was involved.

AARON: Shh! Focus. This is the big moment. Now move your lips in a circle. *(Sees Sister Rita coming and ducks out of sight.)*

SAM: *(He moves his lips around.)* Mmm. Do I put my tongue in her mouth? Aaron? *(Opens his eyes, high-pitched.)* Sister Rita! Hi!

Little Sister, Big Trouble

by Janet B. Milstein and Diana Xin

Luke: 16 to 18 years old, male
Ryan: 16 to 18 years old, male

Luke approaches Ryan in the hall to find out about Ryan's date.

LUKE: There you are, man. I've been looking everywhere for you. Sooo? How'd it go?

RYAN: *(Nervous.)* Um. How did what go?

LUKE: The date! If you ditch the game for a date, tell me you at least got to first base.

RYAN: Well, Luke, that's the thing. I, um—

LUKE: You got nowhere, huh? I keep telling you, man, you just gotta go for it. Girls can smell it when you're afraid. And, Ryan, the only deodorant for fear is confidence.

RYAN: It was Lily! I went on a date with Lily!

LUKE: What? Lily, my sister, Lily?!

RYAN: Please don't hit me.

LUKE: You put the moves on my little sister?!

RYAN: She put the moves on me! *(Off Luke's look.)* OK, hit me. But please don't hit my face. I like my face. Lily likes my face.

LUKE: You get her name out of your filthy mouth!

RYAN: I'm sorry!

LUKE: I can't believe you, man. You're my best friend! She's my baby sister! That is exceedingly uncool.

RYAN: But, Luke! I didn't do anything!

LUKE: So you're saying nothing happened?

RYAN: Well . . . I wouldn't say . . . It was her! She lunged at me!

LUKE: What?!

RYAN: She trapped me in the car. I couldn't escape! She is scary strong.

LUKE: My baby sister attacked *you*? She's five-two! And a girl!

RYAN: You don't know your sister, man. She's an animal! I have scars!

LUKE: Are you calling my sister a . . . ? I think I'm going to hit you now.

RYAN: Don't hit me! Help me! She wants to go out again. She wants to be *(Whispers.)* sweethearts. *(Normal voice.)* You gotta stop her. I'm scared.

LUKE: Wait, wait. So, you go out with my sister and just use her and dump her?

RYAN: I didn't—She—Wait! You just said—

LUKE: Shut it! Don't you dare break my sister's heart! You're taking her to the prom. And you better come over Sunday for dinner. Our family sticks together. *(Exits.)*

RYAN: Family? *(Sinks to a kneeling or sitting position.)* God help me.

Mesmerized

by Janet B. Milstein

Tyler: 13 to 15 years old, male
Michael: 13 to 15 years old, male

Tyler and Michael stare ahead, checking out the beauty in front of them.

TYLER: My God!

MICHAEL: She's good-looking.

TYLER: She's beyond that, dude. She's perfect.

MICHAEL: Indeed.

TYLER: Check out that body.

MICHAEL: I'm checking it out. Trust me.

TYLER: She's smoking.

MICHAEL: Flawless.

TYLER: Sweet.

MICHAEL: I'm in love.

TYLER: Dude, how old do you think she is?

MICHAEL: Who cares?

TYLER: Don't be an idiot. Seriously, how old?

MICHAEL: Hmm. I'd say nineteen, twenty.

TYLER: No way. She's older than that.

MICHAEL: No she's not.

TYLER: Yes she is. She's at least twenty-five.

MICHAEL: Are you crazy? She's not *that* old.

TYLER: Don't get me wrong. I like older, but she is twenty-five or more.

MICHAEL: Oh yeah? If you're so sure, why don't you ask?

TYLER: Are you stupid? I'm not gonna ask.

MICHAEL: Why? Cause you know you're wrong and I'm right?

TYLER: No, because you just don't ask that. It'll make me sound like a doofus.

MICHAEL: You are a doofus.

TYLER: Shut up.

MICHAEL: Chicken! *(He makes chicken noises.)*

TYLER: I'm not afraid, you idiot!

MICHAEL: Fine. Then ask. I dare you.

TYLER: No way!

MICHAEL: OK, I double dare you!

TYLER: Fine!

MICHAEL: Fine!

TYLER: OK! *(Beat. He takes a step forward nervously.)* Excuse me? My friend right there was just wondering . . . um . . . how old's that car?

No Girls Allowed

by Josh Darby

Jim: 13 to 15 years old, male
Dylan: 13 to 15 years old, male

Jim and Dylan are in a clubhouse. Jim stands.

JIM: Welcome to this week's meeting of the No Girls Allowed
Club. Role call: John? *(No answer.)* Steve? *(No answer.)*
Dylan?

DYLAN: Here.

JIM: Billy? *(No answer.)* Ted? *(No answer.)*

DYLAN: Jim . . . uhh . . . Jim?

JIM: What is it, Dylan? I'm taking role.

DYLAN: There's no one else here.

JIM: What? Where is everyone?

DYLAN: Well, John is ice skating with Beth, Steve went to the
fair with Mary, Billy is at Gina's, and Ted is down the street
at the Dairy Queen.

JIM: Did he forget about our meeting?

DYLAN: No, he's there with Crystal.

JIM: That's not cool. We've all been members of the No Girls
Allowed Club since first grade, and the only rule is No Girls.

DYLAN: But they all have girlfriends now.

JIM: Fine, anyone with a girlfriend is no longer allowed in the
No Girls Allowed Club. Just me and you, Dylan.

DYLAN: Actually, I have a date too. Just wanted to stop by and tell you that no one was going to be here. See you later, Jim.

(Dylan exits.)

JIM: I hate girls.

Prom Predicament

by Jill Puleo

Sean: 15 to 18 years old, male
Ty: 15 to 18 years old, male

Ty and Sean talk about the prom.

SEAN: If you could bring any celebrity to the prom, who would you bring?

TY: Vanessa Hudgens. Hands down. She's hot.

SEAN: Vanessa Hudgens? From *High School Musical*? You watched that?

TY: The music is rockin'.

SEAN: Riiight. OK. So, let's say you found out she was related to you. Would you still take her?

TY: How related?

SEAN: How's she related to you?

TY: Yeah, like, I mean, how much? Like a tenth cousin once removed or like a secret sister my mother gave up for adoption?

SEAN: Like first-cousin related.

TY: Ooh. Tough call.

SEAN: But she's your first cousin! What is there to think about?

TY: Well, there's her legs, her voice, the racy photos . . . she's hot.

SEAN: What? Photos? Where?

TY: Hey, she's *my* fantasy girl. Hands off.

SEAN: Fine, geez. But remember, she's your first cousin now. So, do you take her, or not?

TY: I gotta say, I'd still take her.

SEAN: Your own cousin?! To the prom?! Dude!

TY: Hey, it's Vanessa-freakin'-Hudgens, man. I would take her, not just to the prom, but, like . . . everywhere—Woodfield Mall, the grocery store, the DMV . . . Seriously, I'd make sure everyone knew I am out with—

SEAN: YOUR COUSIN?!

TY: Hey, man, what can I say? Genetic similarities be damned, she's *hot.*

SEAN: *(Sheepish, in agony.)* Well . . . I'm glad you feel that way, man. Cause my mom is making me take my cousin Katie to the prom.

TY: Oh, dude, that's nasty!

Sabotaged

by Janet B. Milstein

Evan: 13 to 18 years old, male
Steve: 13 to 18 years old, male

*Evan and Steve are at a speech tournament. They were com-
peting in the dramatic duo event. They just walked out of the
judging room after a terrible performance.*

EVAN: Steve, hold up!

STEVE: Get away from me.

EVAN: C'mon! I'm sorry. OK?

STEVE: We came in last, Evan! Because of you! There's no way
we're going to regionals now!

EVAN: I know our speech competition was important, but it
wasn't my fault I ruined it!

STEVE: You didn't speak! Who else's fault could it be?!

EVAN: Marisa Ford. She winked at me—right when I was about
to start—and whoosh—everything in my mind just left. Except her.

STEVE: Evan, I'm a dude, I get distracted, too. But not when
we've practiced and prepped for months!

EVAN: But Steve—

STEVE: No, no! I broke your girl-straction. I elbowed you!

EVAN: I know, and I tried really hard to remember my lines.
But then Marisa leaned in, and she had this low-cut top on,
and, and—what was I supposed to do?

STEVE: Focus!

EVAN: I was defenseless!

STEVE: Evan, I warned you that the other teams play dirty!

EVAN: I thought you meant they don't bathe.

STEVE: No! They plot to destroy. Dude, you were sabotaged!

EVAN: You think she purposely distracted me so we'd lose?

STEVE: Yes! And we did!

EVAN: Maybe. Because right when you slapped me on the back, Marisa slowly licked her lips—that's why I sort of coughed out the word *hot*.

STEVE: Face it, you lost our trophy to a cold-blooded, calculating—albeit good-looking—rival.

EVAN: I think we should tell the judges and have some sort of do-over.

STEVE: Dream on, Distracto.

EVAN: Seriously. To prove that she purposely threw me off. And they should make Marisa do those things to me again . . . *(He gets distracted at the thought of it.)* and again and again!

STEVE: And he's off.

Team Spirit

by Jill Puleo

Ben: 15 to 18 years old, male
Mitch: 15 to 18 years old, male

Ben enters the detention room and takes a seat next to Mitch.

BEN: Hey.

MITCH: Hey.

BEN: You got detention too, huh?

MITCH: Yeah.

BEN: What did you do?

MITCH: Running in the halls. I was late for practice. It's a big
school.

BEN: *(Shrugs.)* So, you play sports or something?

MITCH: Yeah. Sort of.

BEN: Sort of? What team are you on?

MITCH: *(Mumbles.)* Drill team.

BEN: Drill team? What's that? ROTC?

MITCH: No . . . *(Quietly.)* It's cheerleading.

BEN: *(Laughs, thinking Mitch is making a joke.)* Cheerleading?
No, seriously, ROTC?

MITCH: No. Cheerleading.

BEN: Cheerleading?! That's not a sport. And it's for girls, unless you're . . .

MITCH: President? George W. Bush was a cheerleader.

BEN: Yeah, well, he sucked as a president.

MITCH: Dude, show some respect. You know how popular you've got to be to become the president?

BEN: *(Shrugging.)* Just enough to sway the electoral college. *(Off Mitch's astonished glance.)* What? I read.

MITCH: Yeah, well, still . . . Drill team has its rewards.

BEN: Dude. Cheerleading? There are better ways to be popular than cheerleading. Way better ways.

MITCH: None that involve catching girls in short skirts.

BEN: *(Immobilized by this image.)* True that. But still . . .

MITCH: Girls. In. Short. Skirts.

BEN: *(Dreamy with lustful thoughts.)* Right . . . right . . . short skirts . . . huh . . .

MITCH: *(To himself.)* Got to remember to lead with that.

Wicked Crush

by Janet B. Milstein and Diana Xin

Gordon: 14 to 16 years old, male
Spencer: 14 to 16 years old, male

Gordon and Spencer are trying to act cool as they talk to Vicky, an offstage girl.

GORDON: Hi, Vicky. You look great.

SPENCER: You look better than great.

GORDON: Yeah, you look sick.

SPENCER: *(To Gordon.)* What?! *(To Vicky.)* Oh . . . yeah! You do.

GORDON: Your dress is, uh, dope. Cool studs.

SPENCER: Definitely. Is that a new nose ring? It really brings out your eyes.

GORDON: *(Gives Spencer a dirty look.)* Yeah! They look darker than dark. They're like vampire dark. You like vampires, right?

SPENCER: *(To Gordon.)* Of course she does! *(To Vicky.)* God. He's so lame. By the way, Vick, those blue streaks in your hair are groovy.

GORDON: Wicked. Totally scene.

SPENCER: *(Gives Gordon a dirty look.)* Cooler than scene. More like . . . unseen. You know, I mean, like, unique unto you?

GORDON: Right. So, anyway, Vicky, there's this party—

SPENCER: At Rueben Goldstein's house—

GORDON: It's this Friday night—

SPENCER: At eight o'clock—

GORDON: His parents are gone, and this emo band's playing—

SPENCER: *(To Gordon.)* They're not emo! They're punk. Ish. *(To Vicky.)* Sort of goth. Or alt.

GORDON: They wear nose rings! You'll like them.

SPENCER: Exactly! They're very good.

GORDON: And so, Vicky, I wanted—

SPENCER: No, Vicky, *I* wanted—

GORDON: To ask you—

SPENCER: If *you* wanted—

GORDON: To go to the party—

GORDON/SPENCER: With *me*?! *(Beat. Both their faces drop.)* You're going with Sledge Botman?

GORDON: *(Beat.)* Your dress is a train wreck.

SPENCER: And your nose ring looks like a wart.

(They turn up their noses and walk away together.)

GORDON: I didn't really like her anyway.

SPENCER: Yeah. I mean, who has blue hair?

Scenes for One Male
and One Female

Authentic Italian

by Mark Carroll

Paul: 16 to 18 years old, male
Beth: 16 to 18 years old, female

Beth and Paul are in Paul's car heading out for their first date.

PAUL: *(Nervous.)* Wow, Beth, you look great tonight.

BETH: Thanks, you too. I'm so excited to find out what the big secret plan is.

PAUL: Well, I figured, it's our first date, and I wanted to take you somewhere special for dinner.

BETH: Aww, that sounds great, Paul. So what place did you pick?

PAUL: *(Pulls into the restaurant and stops the car. Says with flourish.)* Olive Garden.

BETH: *(Chuckles.)* Um, Olive Garden? But . . . we got all dressed up. Don't you want to go somewhere nicer?

PAUL: *(Incredulous.)* What's nicer than Olive Garden?!

BETH: Oh, I don't know, maybe that new steakhouse or . . . sushi?

PAUL: *(Getting defensive.)* Do those places have unlimited salad and breadsticks? I don't think so!

BETH: I don't know if we really need unlimited salad and breadsticks.

PAUL: Well, you clearly don't understand what unlimited means.

BETH: I know what unlimited—

PAUL: How about endless; do you know what endless means? Because there are endless possibilities with the Never-Ending Pasta Bowl! You could have spaghetti with marinara, or angel hair with alfredo, or penne with sundried tomato.

BETH: Look, I just think this place is kind of cheesy.

PAUL: You bet it's cheesy. Cheesy and delicious!

BETH: I meant the whole thing. It's so tacky and fake!

PAUL: What?! Olive Garden is *authentic Italian*. It's like being in a Tuscan villa!

BETH: It's a *chain*! It's a Sunday-afternoon-take-the-family-to-a-crappy-fake-wannabe Italian restaurant to stifle the boredom. This is our first date! It's supposed to be special!

PAUL: *(Hushed.)* Wow. Clearly, I made a mistake.

BETH: *(Relieved.)* Thank you. So, what do you say to some juicy sirloin steaks?

PAUL: I meant, I was mistaken about you. I thought you were someone with taste. Obviously, you don't have the palate for Olive Garden. Now, I see, we have nothing in common.

BETH: *(Shocked, hurt, then recovering.)* You're right. You're stubborn, selfish, obsessive, and your "taste" in food sucks. *(Beat.)* I'd like to go home, now, please.

PAUL: Fine. But, while we're here, let's at least get some Olive Garden takeout.

BETH: *(Covers her face and moans.)* Uhh!

Backstage Pass

by David-Matthew Barnes

Tammy: 13 to 18 years old, female
Evan: 13 to 18 years old, male

Best friends Evan and Tammy are trying to convince a very strict security guard to let them backstage to meet their favorite band. Both of them talk directly to the offstage security guard.

TAMMY: You're probably wondering why we're back again.

EVAN: Yeah, especially since you already told us no.

TAMMY: But we never take no for an answer. Right, Evan?

EVAN: No. I mean yes. I mean you're right, Tammy.

TAMMY: You seem like a nice man. *(To Evan.)* Doesn't this security guard seem like a nice man?

EVAN: Well, actually, sir, you scare me. But that's only because you seem so nice.

TAMMY: And we're nice, too.

EVAN: Very nice.

TAMMY: And we really love Sour Kitten.

EVAN: We have every one of their CDs.

TAMMY: I'd let you listen to them on my iPod but . . .

EVAN: She sold her iPod so that we could buy tickets to the concert.

TAMMY: Even though my mother really needed the money for . . .

EVAN: A plane ticket to Indianapolis for . . .

TAMMY: A little blind girl that only Jesus can save.

TAMMY/EVAN: We're really nice people.

TAMMY: So, I think you should let us backstage because . . .

EVAN: We look good. I mean, we deserve it.

TAMMY: Because we are Sour Kitten's number-one fans.

EVAN: Sir, I know you're only doing your job.

TAMMY: And you're really good at it, too.

EVAN: An excellent job!

TAMMY: You should get a raise.

EVAN: Who is your supervisor?

TAMMY: *(Falls to her knees.)* Please, please, please. I'll sell you anything you want. My class ring. My cell phone. My sister! *(She pulls Evan down to the ground with her.)*

EVAN: I don't have a sister but you're welcome to my step-mother.

TAMMY: *(Beat.)* What? Only one of us can go backstage? *(She jumps up and shoves Evan down, then bolts.)* See you, Evan!

Brother and Sister

by Jennifer Kirkeby

Zach: 16 to 17 years old, male, brother to Jana
Jana: 16 to 17 years old, female, sister to Zach

Zach needs a favor from Jana.

ZACH: How's my favorite sister?

JANA: I'm your *only* sister.

ZACH: That's true, but even if I had another one, you'd still be my favorite.

JANA: What do you want?

ZACH: Why do you think I want something?

JANA: Because whenever you tell me that I'm your favorite sister, it always means that you want something. So, what is it?

ZACH: You seem stressed or something. Are you still mad at me for losing your cell phone?

JANA: You dropped it in the toilet. There's a big difference.

ZACH: I know, and I'm really sorry. It was a very unfortunate accident.

JANA: Whatever.

ZACH: Look at it this way—now you'll be getting a brand-new phone.

JANA: But think of all the calls that I'm missing in the meantime!

ZACH: You can borrow mine.

JANA: Really? OK, thanks.

ZACH: If you'll just do one tiny favor for me.

JANA: I *knew* it! What is it?

ZACH: Can I borrow your car?

JANA: What for?

ZACH: I have a date tonight.

JANA: You liar! With who?

ZACH: Maddie.

JANA: Maddie, as in my best friend, Maddie? You're kidding, right?

ZACH: No.

JANA: You two are total opposites!

ZACH: You know what they say about opposites . . .

JANA: This isn't happening. Besides, Maddie told me that she's going to the movies tonight with this really cute guy with a great personality.

(Zach smiles.)

JANA: Aughhh!

The Contingency Plan

by Adam Simon

Spencer: 16 to 18 years old, male
Mackenzie: 16 to 18 years old, female

Spencer and Mackenzie are dating, and Mackenzie is spending the night at Spencer's while his parents are out of town.

SPENCER: So, let's go over the plan again.

MACKENZIE: Spencer, I told you my parents aren't going to call, besides—

SPENCER: We need the contingency plan in case they do. I created a contingency plan. If you mock the contingency plan, you mock me and everything I stand for.

MACKENZIE: Fine. I gave them your house number and told them it was Callie's number.

SPENCER: Right, and if they call?

MACKENZIE: If they call your house, you're going to pick up and pretend to be Callie's dad.

SPENCER: Affirmative, and what's your assignment?

MACKENZIE: I turn on the TV to a game.

SPENCER: Right, continue.

MACKENZIE: Can't we just—

SPENCER: Continue!

MACKENZIE: Fine. You need to calm down. OK, you'll say you need to get off the phone because it's an important—

SPENCER: Critical!

MACKENZIE: It's a critical point in the game.

SPENCER: Exactly. It's not perfect, but it'll do.

MACKENZIE: Chill out. If they call, they'll call my cell phone. You don't need to worry—

SPENCER: What channel is ESPN?

MACKENZIE: I don't know.

SPENCER: You didn't even read my e-mail about the plan, did you?

MACKENZIE: I read it.

SPENCER: But you obviously didn't even open the attachment. ESPN was covered in detail in the attachment. This will never work. I can't take this kind of pressure. I'm trying to keep the whole operation together, and you aren't pulling your weight!

MACKENZIE: Well, pardon me!

SPENCER: I think you should go home.

MACKENZIE: Spencer, relax. Tonight is gonna be great, it's gonna be just us and—

SPENCER: It's not gonna be "just us." It'll be you, me, and the constant threat of a carefully laid-out plan collapsing around us featuring a guest appearance by your enraged, unstable father! Next time, we'll plan this out better. There will be diagrams. Be prepared!

Ditched for the Dead

by Janet B. Milstein and Diana Xin

Sean: 16 to 18 years old, male
Margaret: 16 to 18 years old, female

Sean and Margaret are standing in the lobby of an emptying movie theater.

SEAN: Come on! *(Leans in to Margaret. She turns away.)* Say something! *(Leans in to Margaret's other side. She turns away again.)* Please, Margaret?

MARGARET: *(Smacking him away.)* Get off of me! I waited two hours for you, Sean! Two hours! The movie is over!

SEAN: I know! I'm sorry! But . . . was it good?

MARGARET: I missed the first half waiting for you! I had to sit in the first row and stare straight up. My neck is killing me.

SEAN: Do you want me to rub it? *(Reaching up to massage her neck.)*

MARGARET: *(Smacking his hand away.)* Do! Not! Touch! You better have a good excuse. I thought you were dead! You better have died!

SEAN: That's not funny. Because, you know what, Margaret? My grandma did! Die. She died! *(Breaks down crying loudly.)*

MARGARET: What?! Oh my God! Are you OK?

SEAN: *(Louder sob.)* Yeah. *(High-pitched, between sobs.)* I'm. Fine.

MARGARET: Sean! What happened?!

SEAN: She fell, and she can't get up. She'll never get up again.

MARGARET: That's awful! I'm so sorry, Sean.

SEAN: Me, too. I loved my grandma Gertie. *(Sniffs sadly.)*

MARGARET: Grandma Gertie?

SEAN: Mmm hmm. She was my favorite! Oh, God! *(Collapses onto Margaret, hugging her.)*

MARGARET: *(Stiff.)* Wow. You really loved her. I can tell, cause you cried this hard THE LAST TIME SHE DIED!

SEAN: *(Stands straight again.)* No—she—she—you—

MARGARET: I sent flowers to her funeral!

SEAN: And she thought they were pretty.

MARGARET: How could you?! You are the worst boyfriend I've ever had! No! No! You . . . are . . . beyond . . . worst. You liar! You stander-upper! You grandma killer!

SEAN: Margaret! Calm down! Please? People are staring! I'm sorry! You're right. I lied. Grandma Gertie didn't die . . . again. The Giants were playing the Colts! I'm sorry! I'll make it up to you! *(To offstage person.)* What are you looking at?!

MARGARET: *(Looks to the same spot. Motions "one second.")* Oh! That's Brian. I met him there in that lonely front row. We shared popcorn. He's nice! And cute. And he's waiting for me. Gotta go. Give my regards to Gertie.

Eau de Betsy

by Diana Xin

Betsy: 16 to 18 years old, female
Danny: 16 to 18 years old, male

Betsy and Danny are on their first date. Betsy gets into the car.

BETSY: Hi, Danny. I'm so excited for our date tonight.

DANNY: Hi, Betsy. Wow. What is *(Sniffs.)* . . . that's a strong . . . *(Sniffs.)* is that your perfume?

BETSY: You like? It's from France.

DANNY: It's um— *(Rubs nose.)* lovely.

BETSY: *(Giggles.)* You're so sweet. What movie are we going to see tonight? I heard that—

DANNY: Aaaachoo!

BETSY: Are you OK?

DANNY: Uh, yeah, I just have a sensitive nose.

BETSY: You are sensitive, Danny! That's what I like about you. That time in math class, when I dropped my pencil and you picked it up for me? I thought you were so nice. Do you still remember that?

DANNY: Um, you mind if I roll down a window?

BETSY: Oh. *(Beat.)* Sure. Go ahead. *(Beat.)* I just want to say—

DANNY: Achoo! Achoo! Achoo!

BETSY: Goodness! Bless you! Anyway, I just— *(Sees him rubbing his eyes.)* watch the road, Danny—I just wanted to let you know how happy I am to be with you.

DANNY: *(Miserably.)* Do you have any Kleenex?

BETSY: No. Not with me.

DANNY: *(Makes a disgusted noise about his sneezing.)* Ugh.

BETSY: What's wrong, Danny? You don't look very happy to be with me.

DANNY: *(Looks at her seriously.)* Betsy, I can't breathe sitting next to you.

BETSY: Oh, Danny. That's so romantic. *(Lays her head on his shoulder.)* I think we're going to have a great time tonight.

DANNY: *(Throat-closing, choking sound.)* Cah-ah-chhh . . . *(Weakly.)* Hospital!

Eggbert

by Diana Xin

Molly: 14 to 18 years old, female
Dexter: 14 to 18 years old, male

Molly and Dexter have been assigned to work on a class project together, but things aren't going well.

MOLLY: You lost our child?!

DEXTER: Lost is a harsh word. It's more like . . . misplaced.

MOLLY: How could you misplace our child?! Our poor, helpless child!

DEXTER: Molly, relax. I think you're taking this just a bit too far. I mean, it's only an egg.

MOLLY: An egg that we're supposed to care for and nurture—not misplace! The one and only egg that is keeping you and me from an F in health!

DEXTER: Yeah . . . there's that. But, come on, we can go to the cafeteria right now. The lunch lady can spare an egg.

MOLLY: It won't be *our* egg! Our egg was special! Our egg had a sticker with serial numbers! Remember?!

DEXTER: Oh. Right. Well, that's a pickle. *(Beat.)* We could say it was egg-napped.

MOLLY: I knew you were an unfit parent. I asked Ms. Larson for full custody, but nooo, she insisted, "Every egg needs its father."

DEXTER: Calm down, Molly. I'll find it. I swear. I'll find our little Eggbert.

MOLLY: Then where is he?!

DEXTER: Don't yell. I can't think under pressure. Help me retrace my steps.

MOLLY: Fine. Where did you last see him?

DEXTER: This morning, by my bed. I got dressed, and I took him downstairs so I wouldn't forget to bring him to school.

MOLLY: *(Sarcastically.)* And that worked!

DEXTER: I put him on the kitchen counter, I went for a run, showered, and then I was late. But my mom made me eat breakfast, so I had some toast and eggs and—

MOLLY: Eggs?

DEXTER: Scrambled. With cheddar and—Oh! Ohhh. *(Horror.)* Oh, no . . .

MOLLY: *(Quiet but deadly.)* You *ate* our baby?

DEXTER: I didn't know! I was so hungry!

MOLLY: Murderer. That's it. I'm asking Ms. Larson for a divorce. You cannibal.

DEXTER: I think I might be sick.

Electioneers

by Adam Simon

Janie: 16 to 18 years old, female
Fin: 16 to 18 years old, male

Janie and Fin are in Janie's parents' study.

JANIE: So what's the plan?

FIN: If we're going to do this, we're going to do it right.

JANIE: I like that plan.

FIN: My sources tell me that the field is wide open.

JANIE: What about Vikram?

FIN: Not running.

JANIE: No way!

FIN: Yes.

JANIE: No *way*!

FIN: Don't make me repeat myself.

JANIE: Wait, how come you're not running?

FIN: Janie, Janie, you're so new to this racket. Last year. Cherry bomb. Third-floor bathroom. Freshman year. Vikram in the lead. Scandalous YouTube clip emerges. I have too many skeletons in my closet.

JANIE: Whoa. You did that? That's intense.

FIN: Politics is a ruthless game. Now, we'll need to build a coalition—

JANIE: You really think I could be class president?

FIN: Absofruitly.

JANIE: Hey! That'll look good on a college application.

FIN: Good? Good? "Good" is when Mrs. Meister shows a movie instead of talking. This would be better than good. How do you feel about doing some photo-ops with nerds?

JANIE: Like, actual nerds or can we just Photoshop it?

FIN: Real, live, in-the-flesh nerds.

JANIE: Do I have to?

FIN: Do you "have to" be class president?

JANIE: Gosh! Politics is harder than I thought.

FIN: No one said it was easy.

JANIE: Uhhh. OK, fine. As long as they don't touch me, breathe on me, or talk to me. I'll just wave and smile.

FIN: Janie! You're more of a natural politician than I thought.

Good Night Kiss

by Diana Xin

Casey: 16 to 18 years old, male
Sarah: 16 to 18 years old, female

Casey and Sarah have just returned from their first date. They are standing outside Sarah's house.

CASEY: *(Nervous.)* I, um, had a great time tonight, Sarah.

SARAH: Me, too. Thanks for the ride home. I love your car.

CASEY: Thanks! Actually, it's my grandma's. But, it will be mine one day.

SARAH: That's nice. *(Edging closer to him. In throatier, flirty voice.)* So, are you going to kiss me good night?

CASEY: Oh. Um, right. OK!

(Sarah leans in, puckering her lips. Casey leans in several times to kiss her but stops.)

CASEY: I feel like I need a breath mint. Do you have a breath mint?

SARAH: Your breath is fine. Come on, Casey. Clock's ticking.

CASEY: *(Tries again but backs off.)* What about ChapStick? Do you have ChapStick?

SARAH: *(In normal voice.)* Casey! My dad will be home any minute. If he finds you here, he will kill you! Do you want to die, Casey? Now kiss me!

CASEY: I can't! I've never kissed a girl before! Ahhh, stupid! Did I really say that out loud?

SARAH: You've never?

CASEY: *(Miserably.)* Never.

SARAH: Oh. Oh, my. That's . . .

CASEY: Pathetic?

SARAH: No. Cute. Don't worry, Casey. I'm going to teach you all about the art of kissing. Now, *(Grabs his shoulders.)* look into my eyes.

CASEY: You have pretty eyes.

SARAH: *(Suddenly grabs and dips him.)* You bet I do.

CASEY: *(Looking both horrified and intrigued.)* I can't believe this is happening.

SARAH: Close your eyes, and— *(Looks up. A beat of horror.)* Daddy! *(Drops Casey to the ground.)*

CASEY: Ow! *(Scrambling up.)* Oh! Hi, Mr. Wilson!

SARAH: Hi, Daddy! You're home! This is not how it looks. Dad! Put down the rake! Daddy—Ohh! Run, Casey, run!

CASEY: *(Takes off and looks back over his shoulder.)* Nice to meet you, Mr. Wilson!

SARAH: *(Calls out to him.)* Call me!

The Lost Car

by Lindsay Price

Murray: 16 to 18 years old, male, brother to Fran
Fran: 13 to 15 years old, female, sister to Murray

Fran and Murray stand in the mall parking lot. Fran is on the phone with the police as they believe Murray's car has been stolen. Murray grabs his head in exaggerated anguish.

MURRAY: *(To himself.)* Breathe. Stay calm. Don't panic.

FRAN: *(On phone.)* I'd like to report a stolen car.

MURRAY: *(Lets out a sob, a moan, and a spasm of dismay.)* Aaaagh—aaagrugah.

FRAN: *(On phone.)* It's my brother's car. *(To Murray.)* You're so lucky I'm here. *(On phone.)* He can't speak at the moment—he's in the throws of distress. A spasm beyond words. He's upset.

MURRAY: *(Whimpers and wrings his hands. Runs in a circle.)* Aaaaaaa-aaaagruagh. Ah. Ah. Ah.

FRAN: *(On phone.)* And truthfully, it isn't my brother's car, it's my dad's, which my brother "borrowed" when he wasn't supposed to. *(To Murray.)* Dad is so going to kill you.

MURRAY: *(Slaps his head in agreement.)* Stupid. Stupid. Stupid!

FRAN: *(On phone.)* Murray's been grounded three times now because he keeps getting speeding tickets. And what ticks me off is, the more he gets in trouble, the more my dad's gonna tighten the reins on me. He already said I can't get my license till I'm seventeen, which is so unfair I can't begin to tell you—

MURRAY: *(Flails his arms at Fran, telling her to "get on with it.")* AAAAAAGGHHH! FOCUS!

FRAN: *(To Murray.)* Sorry. *(On phone.)* Could you send someone out as quickly as possible? Not that it really matters; he's only going to live till Dad finds out. *(To Murray.)* What do you want your last meal to be? Ice cream?

MURRAY: *(Agrees in a pathetic, childlike tone.)* Chocolate?

FRAN: We're in the parking garage next to the Seacrest Mall. Level C, spot 17.

MURRAY: Uhhhh— *(In midgroan and exaggerated flailing, Murray stops.)* We're where?

FRAN: C17.

MURRAY: C17?

FRAN: Isn't that where you parked?

MURRAY: I said *D17*!!

FRAN: *(To person on phone. Beat.)* Never mind.

Making the Cut

by John Michael Manship

Ben: 14 to 16 years old, male
Sara: 14 to 16 years old, female

Ben, captain of the Frisbee team, has to cut Sara from the team, but he also wants to take the opportunity to ask her out. Sara knows how to manipulate him with her beauty.

BEN: Good practice, Sara.

SARA: Oh, hi, Brad . . .

BEN: Ben . . .

SARA: Brennan. Sorry.

BEN: The captain . . . of the Frisbee team.

SARA: Right.

BEN: Ben.

SARA: Right.

BEN: I wanted to ask you . . . tell you, actually. The other captains . . . I'm supposed to tell you. How are you . . . feeling. . . about Frisbee?

SARA: I love it. I'm having so much fun. I don't catch it much—

BEN: No.

SARA: But I really have a lot of fun. I love the exercise and the people. I've made so many friends.

BEN: Yeah. Me, too. So . . . are you . . . going to keep playing? I mean, we have to decide who's going to compete, and well, you know it's completely voluntary. We're not really allowed to cut anybody. Just . . . ah . . . are you . . .

SARA: You're cute, Ben. You stutter a lot.

BEN: Am I? Thanks. Look, I don't really want to do this, it's just . . . the other captains and stuff . . . and you've never played before . . . and you don't come to practice much . . .

SARA: I know. I've been really busy. You've been so understanding. You guys are so sweet.

BEN: Really? Sweet?

SARA: Yeah.

BEN: Are you doing anything on Friday night?

SARA: I have a boyfriend. *(Pause.)* What did you want to tell me?

BEN: You're terrible at Frisbee. The captains want you to quit the team.

The Messenger

by Steven Schutzman

David: 13 to 14 years old, male
Katie: 13 to 14 years old, female

David walks up to Katie.

DAVID: Uh . . .

KATIE: Hi.

DAVID: Uh . . . This wasn't my idea.

KATIE: OK.

DAVID: They like sent me over here.

KATIE: So, you're their slave?

DAVID: Yeah. Like. No.

KATIE: OK.

DAVID: More like a messenger.

KATIE: OK. What's the message?

DAVID: I don't know.

KATIE: You don't know the message?

DAVID: Uh . . . I forgot.

KATIE: You're not a very good messenger.

DAVID: I know. I know I'm not.

KATIE: So, what's your name?

DAVID: David.

KATIE: So, David, do you want to go back and find out what the message is again?

DAVID: Yeah. No. Actually, there is no message.

KATIE: Oh.

DAVID: And I'm not a messenger.

KATIE: Oh.

DAVID: It was more like, you know, a dare.

KATIE: A dare? You mean, you didn't really want to do it?

DAVID: Uh . . . Uh . . . No . . . Look, this is me talking now . . .

KATIE: You?

DAVID: Yeah . . . Me . . . Not them . . . David . . . Talking . . . To you . . . You see, I wanted to come over and say hi to you, and I didn't know how, so I said that other stuff.

KATIE: You just wanted to say hi to me?

DAVID: Yeah. Hi. That's the message. Hi.

KATIE: Hi, David. I'm Katie.

DAVID: Hi. Yeah. Hi, Katie. Cool. Let's ditch those guys.

KATIE: OK.

(They walk off.)

Prom Date

by Ross Evans

Ryan: 16 years old, male
Lindsay: 16 years old, female

Ryan and Lindsay are standing outside their lockers in between classes.

RYAN: Hi.

LINDSAY: Hi.

    (Silence.)

LINDSAY: Ryan?

RYAN: Lindsay.

    (Silence.)

LINDSAY: Ryan, you asked me to meet you at your locker.

RYAN: I did.

LINDSAY: So what do you want?

RYAN: I . . . I . . . Can you stop looking at me?

LINDSAY: What?

RYAN: Can you not look at me with your eyes?

LINDSAY: You asked me to meet you here, so you can tell me to stop looking at you with my eyes?

RYAN: Oh no, God no. It's just . . . I have trouble talking to you when you look at me with your eyes. They're this really pretty green, and when I look at them, I feel like I'm gonna throw up in your face.

LINDSAY: Oh, gross, but thanks. I guess.

RYAN: Can you like turn around?

LINDSAY: Sure.

> *(Lindsay turns around. Ryan smells her hair.)*

RYAN: Forgot about the hair.

LINDSAY: What?

> *(Lindsay turns around. Ryan looks in her eyes and covers his mouth like he is about to throw up.)*

RYAN: TURN AROUND! TURN AROUND!

LINDSAY: Sorry.

RYAN: Listen, Lindsay, I just . . . well . . . I have to ask . . . well, beg you . . . no, ask you . . . I mean . . . I have to . . . Oh, sd.

LINDSAY: Yes, I'll go to prom with you.

RYAN: How did you know?

LINDSAY: Why else would you ask me here?

RYAN: I . . . I don't know. Then why did you make me . . .

LINDSAY: Cause you're cute when you're nervous.

> *(Lindsay kisses Ryan on the cheek and exits.)*

Road Rage, Really

by Lindsay Price

Tess: 16 to 17 years old, female
Nate: 14 to 15 years old, male

Nate tries to explain to Tess that her driving attitude might be a little over the top. Nate and Tess sit side by side in the front seat of a car.

TESS: *(To another car.)* Hel-lo! If you hang up your cell phone, maybe you could watch the road! Hang up hang up hang up! *(To Nate. She completely changes her tone.)* Do you need a ride after school?

NATE: *(Terrified.)* No. Uh-uh. I'm going to take the bus.

TESS: Why? We hate the bus. The bus smells.

NATE: It's not that bad. Really. I hardly notice.

TESS: *(Yelling.)* Where'd you learn to drive, moron? *(Changing tone.)* I finally get to drive and you want to take the bus? *(Changing tone.)* Did you get your license out of a Cracker Jack box?!

NATE: *(Blurting out.)* I'd rather ride the bus than drive with you!

TESS: What?! Really?

NATE: You have road rage. Really.

TESS: *(Very mild.)* I do not. Road rage? Come on, I'm just expressing myself. *(Yelling.)* It's not nice to cut in front, Jacko!

NATE: You're going to express yourself into a heart attack, and I don't want to be in the car when it happens. No offense.

TESS: Don't be so dramatic. I'm just pointing it out. I'm calm. And trustworthy and kind. Who organizes the food drive at Christmas? Huh? Who?

NATE: There's no driving at the food drive.

TESS: And *who* did Sister Katherine entrust to run the peer mediation group for three years straight?

NATE: It's not the same thing! You get in a car and you get all . . . scary!

TESS: Three years. Three calm, sweet, loving years.

NATE: Fine. You're a beautiful human being. The planet couldn't do without you. The highway could. But, I am grateful to be in your presence.

TESS: Better. And you'll ride home with me after school?

NATE: *(Wincing.)* OK.

TESS: Great! *(Yelling.)* Stay in your lane, you pea-brained butter ball!

NATE: You might have to rethink that three-year record.

TESS: What? Why?

NATE: That was Sister Katherine.

The Trouble with Love

by Diana Xin

Gretchen: 14 to 16 years old, female
Billy: 14 to 16 years old, male

Billy and Gretchen are in a relationship and have landed themselves in detention.

GRETCHEN: I can't believe this. I have never been in detention before. This is so embarrassing.

BILLY: Hey, don't worry. I've done this tons of times. It's all chill.

GRETCHEN: It is not "chill." We are in major trouble. I can't believe you passed that note to me.

BILLY: Well, you should have grabbed it from me before the teacher saw and took it away. I only passed the note to tell you I left a surprise for you in your locker.

GRETCHEN: Do not tell me you're the reason my locker is covered in toxic blue paint.

BILLY: I nicked it from art class for you. You said you wanted to paint. Did it spill or something?

GRETCHEN: It leaked all over my books. I have to pay for damaging school property. Thanks a lot.

BILLY: I was just trying to do something nice for you since you let me cheat off your science test.

GRETCHEN: What?! I never let you cheat off me!

BILLY: Yeah, you did. You moved your arm over so I could see your answers.

GRETCHEN: I was fixing my hair!

BILLY: Oh. *(Disappointed.)* I thought you were being sweet.

GRETCHEN: *(Moans in anguish.)* My academic record is ruined forever! I'm never going to Harvard now. I hate you! It's over. We're done.

BILLY: No! Really? But . . . you're the best girlfriend I've ever had!

GRETCHEN: *(Touched.)* Really?

BILLY: Yeah. I told you in the note.

GRETCHEN: You wrote that?

BILLY: I also wrote that you're the smartest girl I've ever met.

GRETCHEN: You're so sweet. I'm so glad we're dating.

BILLY: Me, too.

(They hug.)

BILLY: So, can you fix your hair during the math test, too?

GRETCHEN: No. But, we are in detention . . . and there's no one else here . . . You know what we can do?

BILLY: *(Leans closer.)* What's that?

GRETCHEN: Our math homework! *(Off his look.)* Come on, I'll teach you the quadratic formula!

Winning Stephanie

by Janet B. Milstein

Stephanie: 14 to 16 years old, female
Ricky: 14 to 16 years old, male

Ricky and Stephanie are friends. Ricky is secretly in love with Stephanie. The scene takes place at school.

STEPHANIE: Hey, Ricky. How are you? Isn't it a beautiful day?

RICKY: It's raining.

STEPHANIE: I know. Isn't it great?

RICKY: Yeah, I've always loved the rain. The clouds, the dark sky, getting all soggy and pruney. What are you so happy about?

STEPHANIE: Oh, I shouldn't say. It's personal. OK, promise not to tell?

RICKY: Scout's honor. If I break my word, I'll probably get struck by lightning.

STEPHANIE: OK, that's good. Evan Coleman asked me out! Do you believe it?

RICKY: Evan Coleman? Stephanie, you do not want to go out with him. Trust me.

STEPHANIE: Why not?

RICKY: Because he bites his toenails and spits them out.

STEPHANIE: Eww! No way.

RICKY: I'm serious—I know. We shared a bunk at summer camp.

STEPHANIE: Summer camp?

RICKY: OK, it was fifth grade—but still, who's to say he ever stopped? Habits like that are not easy to break. Do you really want to kiss him knowing where his mouth is at night?

STEPHANIE: Well I—

RICKY: Besides, everyone knows he just got dumped by Jenny Freemont. He's on the rebound, and you're his . . . bound, so to speak.

STEPHANIE: He told me he's totally over her. Plus, he confessed that he's always wanted to date me.

RICKY: Oh, c'mon. Then he would have asked you out before. Look, he'll only use you and drop you the second Jenny wants him back.

STEPHANIE: No, he said . . . I mean . . . you really think so?

RICKY: You deserve someone way better than that.

STEPHANIE: Right. Like who?

RICKY: Like . . . me, for example. I'm available.

STEPHANIE: *(Sarcastically.)* You, available? No kidding?

RICKY: Yep. No rebound stuff going on here. And I've never, ever chewed my toenails. Not once.

STEPHANIE: Later. *(She starts to walk away.)*

RICKY: Steph, wait! I was just getting to my really good qualities!

Permissions

ALL IN THE SHAKE by Lindsay Price. © 2009 by Lindsay Price. Printed by permission of the author. All inquiries should be addressed to www.theatrefolk.com.

ALMOST FAMOUS by Monica Flory. © 2009 by Monica Flory. Printed by permission of the author. All inquiries should be addressed to www.monicaflory.com.

AUTHENTIC ITALIAN by Mark Carroll. © 2009 by Mark Carroll. Printed by permission of the author. All inquiries should be addressed to mrcarroll418@yahoo.com.

BACKSTAGE PASS by David-Matthew Barnes. © 2009 by David-Matthew Barnes. Printed by permission of the author. All inquiries should be addressed to dmatthewbarnes@gmail.com.

BROTHER AND SISTER by Jennifer Kirkeby. © 2009 by Jennifer Kirkeby. Printed by permission of the author. All inquiries should be addressed to jenk4@comcast.net.

CARING OLDER BROTHER by Matt Fotis. © 2009 by Matt Fotis. Printed by permission of the author. All inquiries should be addressed to shantz100@msn.com.

COLLATERAL by Janet B. Milstein. © 2009 by Janet B. Milstein. Printed by permission of the author. All inquiries should be addressed to www.janetmilstein.com.

THE CONTINGENCY PLAN by Adam Simon. © 2009 by Adam Simon. Printed by permission of the author. All inquiries should be addressed to adamsimon@gmail.com.

THE DATE ESCAPE by Monica Flory. © 2009 by Monica Flory. Printed by permission of the author. All inquiries should be addressed to www.monicaflory.com.

DITCHED FOR THE DEAD by Janet B. Milstein and Diana Xin. © 2009 by Janet B. Milstein and Diana Xin. Printed by permission of the authors. All inquiries should be addressed to Janet B. Milstein at www.janetmilstein.com and Diana Xin at dandan.xin@gmail.com.

EAU DE BETSY by Diana Xin. © 2009 by Diana Xin. Printed by permission of the author. All inquiries should be addressed to dandan.xin@gmail.com.

EGGBERT by Diana Xin. © 2009 by Diana Xin. Printed by permission of the author. All inquiries should be addressed to dandan.xin@gmail.com.

ELECTIONEERS by Adam Simon. © 2009 by Adam Simon. Printed by permission of the author. All inquiries should be addressed to adamsimon@gmail.com.

FOOD FIGHT by Elaine Tuman. © 2009 by Elaine Tuman. Printed by permission of the author. All inquiries should be addressed to eltuman@hotmail.com.

FREEDOM by Erin Austin. © 2009 by Erin Austin. Printed by permission of the author. All inquiries should be addressed to erinlaustin@gmail.com.

GET YOUR CHEER IN GEAR by Diana Xin. © 2009 by Diana Xin. Printed by permission of the author. All inquiries should be addressed to dandan.xin@gmail.com.

GNOME-CALLER by Barbara Lhota and Janet B. Milstein. © 2009 by Barbara Lhota and Janet B. Milstein. Printed by permission of the authors. All inquiries should be addressed to Barbara Lhota at www.barbaralhota.com and Janet B. Milstein at www.janetmilstein.com.

GOOD NIGHT KISS by Diana Xin. © 2009 by Diana Xin. Printed by permission of the author. All inquiries should be addressed to dandan.xin@gmail.com.

HAPPILY OGRE AFTER by Lindsay Price. © 2009 by Lindsay Price. Printed by permission of the author. All inquiries should be addressed to www.theatrefolk.com.

HE'S SO . . . ! by John McGarvie. © 2009 by John McGarvie. Printed by permission of the author. All inquiries should be addressed to jgmcgarvie@aol.com.

THE HIGHER FIVE by Adam Simon. © 2009 by Adam Simon. Printed by permission of the author. All inquiries should be addressed to adamsimon@gmail.com.

THE HITCHHIKERS by Edith Weiss. © 2009 by Edith Weiss. Printed by permission of the author. All inquiries should be addressed to www.edithweiss.com.

I'LL DIE by Elayne Heilveil. © 2009 by Elayne Heilveil. Printed by permission of the author. All inquiries should be addressed to elaynerh@aol.com.

INSIDE MAN by Matt Van Tassel. © 2009 by Matt Van Tassel. Printed by permission of the author. All inquiries should be addressed to mvantas@gmail.com.

JAMBALAYA'S JALOPIES by Lindsay Price. © 2009 by Lindsay Price. Printed by permission of the author. All inquiries should be addressed to www.theatrefolk.com.

KILLER COOKIE by Lindsay Price. © 2009 by Lindsay Price. Printed by permission of the author. All inquiries should be addressed to www.theatrefolk.com.

KISSING 101 by Barbara Lhota. © 2009 by Barbara Lhota. Printed by permission of the author. All inquiries should be addressed to www.barbaralhota.com.

LITTLE SISTER, BIG TROUBLE by Janet B. Milstein and Diana Xin. © 2009 by Janet B. Milstein and Diana Xin. Printed by permission of the authors. All inquiries should be addressed Janet B. Milstein at www.janetmilstein.com and Diana Xin at dandan.xin@gmail.com.

About the Editor

JANET B. MILSTEIN is an actor, award-winning acting instructor, private acting coach, best-selling author, and series editor. She received her MFA in Acting from SUNY Binghamton in New York and her BA in Theatre with Distinction from the University of Delaware. Janet has written and cowritten several produced screenplays and plays, directed and cast both theater and film, and actively contributes to the theatrical community. She was a founding member and the Artistic Director of Symposium Theatre Company in Chicago. She is currently a co-organizer of Filmmakers in Action and a proud member of Women In Film.

Janet has an extensive acting background in both theater and film. She has performed in more than fifty plays and films in New York, Chicago, Atlanta, Milwaukee, and more. Most recently, Janet has been writing, producing, and performing in independent film, as well as developing a one-person show.

Janet has been teaching acting at studios and schools, universities, and workshops around the country for the past fourteen years. During this time, she has developed a career as a private acting coach. She trains beginning and professional actors in monologues, cold reading, scene study, career counseling, and audition preparation for admission to university theater programs. Janet is listed in *The Book: An Actor's Guide to Chicago* under "Acting Coaches." She can also be found at www.smithandkraus.com under "Meet Our Authors" and on her website at www.janetmilstein.com. Janet offers specialized acting workshops nationally and oversees a number of projects for Smith and Kraus.

Other Books by Janet B. Milstein

Author

Cool Characters for Kids: 71 One-Minute Monologues, Ages 4–12.

The Ultimate Audition Book for Teens: 111 One-Minute Monologues.

Winners' Competition Series Volume 1: Award-winning, 60-Second Comic Monologues, Ages 4 to 12.

Winners' Competition Series Volume 3: Award-winning, 60-Second Comic Monologues, Ages 13 to 18.

Coauthor

Forensics Series, Volume 1: Duo Practice and Competition: Thirty-five 8–10 Minute Original Comedic Plays by Barbara Lhota and Janet B. Milstein.

Forensics Series, Volume 2: Duo Practice and Performance: Thirty-five 8–10 Minute Original Dramatic Scenes by Barbara Lhota and Janet B. Milstein.

Series Editor

Audition Arsenal for Women in Their 20s: 101 Monologues by Type, 2 Minutes and Under.

Audition Arsenal for Men in Their 20s: 101 Monologues by Type, 2 Minutes and Under.

Audition Arsenal for Women in Their 30s: 101 Monologues by Type, 2 Minutes and Under.

Audition Arsenal for Men in Their 30s: 101 Monologues by Type, 2 Minutes and Under.

Forensics Series, Volume 3: Duo Practice and Competition: Thirty-five 8–10 Minute Original Comedic Plays for 2 Females by Ira Brodsky and Barbara Lhota.

Forensics Series, Volume 4: Duo Practice and Competition: Thirty-five 8–10 Minute Original Dramatic Plays for 2 Females by Ira Brodsky and Barbara Lhota.

Winners'Competition Series Volume 2: Award-winning, 90-Second Comic Scenes, Ages 4 to 12.

Want a Workshop?

JANET B. MILSTEIN offers various acting workshops locally and nationally. For information on workshops, please visit Janet's website at www.janetmilstein.com or e-mail Janet at Act4You@msn.com.